The Tender Heart

A Buddhist Response to Suffering

2007
Lantern Books
One Union Square West
Suite 201
New York, NY 10003

Library of Congress Cataloging-in-Publication Data

Yifa.
The tender heart : a Buddhist response to suffering / Venerable Yifa.
p. cm.
ISBN-13: 978-1-59056-111-9 (alk. paper)
ISBN-10: 1-59056-111-2 (alk. paper)
1. Suffering—Religious aspects—Buddhism. 2. Buddhism—Doctrines. I. Title.
BQ4235.Y52 2007
294.3'422—dc22
2007020738

Lantern Books has elected to print this title on Legacy TB, a 100% post-consumer recycled paper, processed chlorine-free. A a result, we have saved the following resources:

10.88 trees, 31.43 lbs of water-borne waste, 4,623 gallons of wastewater, 512 lbs of solid waste, 1,007 lbs of net greenhouse gases, and 7,709,912 BTUs of energy.

As part of Lantern Books' commitment to the environment we have joined the Green Press Initiative, a nonprofit organization supporting publishers in using fiber that is not sourced from ancient or endangered forests. We hope that you, the reader, will support Lantern and the GPI in our endeavor to preserve the ancient forests and the natural systems on which all life depends. One way is to buy books that cost a little more but make a positive commitment to the environment not only in their words, but in the paper that they are written on.

For more information, visit www.greenpressinitiative.org.

The Tender Heart

A Buddhist Response to Suffering

Venerable Yifa

New York · Lantern Books
A Division of Booklight Inc.

Life with suffering and happiness
Is full;
Life with success and failure
Is reasonable;
Life with gain and loss
Is fair;
Life with birth and death
Is natural.

—Venerable Master Hsing Yun
  in 42. *Humble Table, Wise Fare*

To Venerable Master Hsing Yun

for teaching me the Dharma

Acknowledgments

I would like to thank the teachers and my colleagues at Fo Guang Shan temple in Taiwan, Hsi Lai temple in Hacienda Heights, and at the University of the West in Rosemead, California, for all their kindness and support over the years. To Marty Krasney, whom I respect and admire a great deal, and who spent considerable time going through the whole manuscript and provided very thoughtful insights on how to improve it, as well as my friends Art DelVesco and Toinette Lippe for their wise comments and cogent criticism, my deepest gratitude. I would also like to acknowledge the support of Robert Oxnam. My thanks also to Zhi-Chuang Liang of Oklahoma University, and to Michael and Rose, who helped me with the transcription of tapes from my series of lectures at university campuses in Oklahoma. And I am also glad to see the growing Buddhist Community in

Oklahoma led by Dr. Wayne Stein and Tomo Koizumi at
Oklahoma Central University. Thanks also to Professor Colin
Blakemore, who provided me with essential information
about Clive Wearing. And my sincere appreciation to Sister
Meg Funk for a sisterhood that runs deeper and truer than
any doctrinal differences. Finally, thanks to Martin Rowe of
Lantern Books for all his help in putting this book together,
and for the encouragement of, and belief in, my work.

Table of Contents

Preface

This book is a revision of a work previously entitled *Safe-guarding the Heart: A Buddhist Response to Suffering and September 11.* That book was written in the months immediately following the destruction of the twin towers of the World Trade Center, a section of the Pentagon, and the jet plane in Pennsylvania on September 11, 2001. When I had originally thought of writing a book, I had intended to discuss Buddhist ideas about the self and the mind as an introduction to Buddhist thought. However, as I explored these ideas in the wake of September 11, the issue of suffering kept on reappearing, and I realized that this core tenet of Buddhism was tied intimately to our understanding of the self and the mind and could form the heart of a new writing project.

Safeguarding the Heart was published a year after the terrible events of that day. For me, Buddhism's constant and unblinking examination of the reasons for suffering is why I felt *Safeguarding the Heart* might be, at the very least, a gesture toward the healing and understanding that needed to take place if we were to learn and grow from the terrible events of that day. I have been gratified by people's responses to the book and their comments on how they found it useful in thinking about what occurred.

Living in the U.S. in the period immediately after those events, I saw how difficult it was to talk about September 11 and what should be done about it without stirring up enormous emotion and blind terror. In the book, I asked some uncompromising questions of what our response to the terrorist attack should be, and hoped that the United States might reach out in such a way that the cycle of suffering and retribution might be broken. The years since have only shown me how important it is that we learn how best to respond to suffering and to act judiciously so we do not compound that suffering more.

Re-reading the book in preparation for this revision, I was struck once again by how shocking the act was. Yet, frankly, given all that has happened since, the horrific events of that September morning seem now only one day in a terrible and seemingly unending series of days where innocent people going about their daily lives are killed by suicide bombers or murderers. Since then, we have passed through the toppling of the Taliban and seen their re-emergence; we have witnessed the ousting of Saddam Hussein and observed the rising up of an insurgency that now seems multi-headed and difficult to contain or even identify, one that is unified only in its cruelty and savagery. Pictures from Abu Ghraib prison have been released, and we have heard about the torture conducted there and at Guantanamo Bay in the name of preserving our freedom. And there have been other events that have captured the world's attention. In 2003, most of the parties in the civil war in the Democratic Republic of Congo finally came to a tentative peace agreement after a decade in which it is estimated that over three million people lost their lives and many others were raped or displaced. In the same year, the conflict in the Darfur region of Sudan began, whereby militia loyal to the Sudanese government prosecuted a systematic campaign of genocide that has seen upward of 400,000 people murdered, many hundreds of thousands forced to become refugees, and fighting that is now spilling over into Chad and the Central African Republic. Somalia fell back into its lawless ways, the Lord's Resistance Army in Uganda continued to abduct children and force them to do terrible things to each other and adults, while famine in Niger and flooding in Ethiopia has left many thousands without food and homes and at the mercy of the elements. Some of these conflicts have come to an end or there is a tentative truce. But no one should be in any doubt that the legacy of that suffering will be felt for generations.

In the United States, in October 2006 a gunman killed as many as ten young girls in an Amish school in southeastern

Pennsylvania, before killing himself; while in April 2007, a mentally disturbed young man killed thirty-two students and teachers at Virginia Tech. In August 2005, nearly two thousand people died in the aftermath of Hurricane Katrina, which forced Americans to face the misery of poverty and degradation in their own backyard in a way that they hadn't had to confront for generations. At the same time, torrential flooding in India killed over a thousand people and left hundreds of thousands homeless. In December 2004, a tsunami off the coast of Indonesia killed some 230,000 people in a matter of hours. In October 2005, an earthquake in Pakistan left 75,000 dead and over three million people homeless, just as the harsh Kashmiri winter was setting in. These are catastrophic events, about which, we might say, we can do nothing, although the poverty of Louisiana existed before Katrina exposed it, and the easy availability of guns in American society can only make random shootings more likely. However, when we consider preventable or treatable conditions, it is worth noting that each year up to three million people around the world, mostly children, die from malaria, two million from tuberculosis, and nearly three million from AIDS.

My aim here it not to diminish the suffering that took place on September 11, 2001. After all, every one of these statistics constitutes one person, with his or her own life and aspirations and needs and desires, and every one of these individuals died individually. However, the events of that day need to be placed in the context of the universal tide of suffering that ebbs and flows over us, whether we are directly or indirectly to blame for its occurrence. There were many tragedies—both collective and individual—before September 11, and as we have seen there were many after it. There will be many more as this book goes to press and is printed, and yet further in the years to come. Suffering is not going to end soon.

I have, therefore, revised *Safeguarding the Heart* to show how we can learn and grow from *every* shocking event and *every* grave illness. I have attempted to explore how we can process the deep emotional pain that lies for decades inside our individual bodies and even cope with that anger and sorrow that lies for centuries within our collective national identities. I explore in general terms the Buddhist ideas of impermanence, conditional existence, the laws of cause and effect, the nature of the mind and self, and karma, and illustrate how they relate to suffering. I also look at some of the means at our disposal to lessen trauma and foster tranquility both within us and in the world around us. As I stated in *Safeguarding the Heart*, my analysis in *The Tender Heart* doesn't aim to speak for all Buddhists in every Buddhist school. It is based instead on my thoughts as a practitioner of Humanistic Buddhism and my experiences as a nun of nearly thirty years.

In times of tragedy, words and religious expressions can seem hopelessly vague and empty. As we discovered in the wake of September 11, calls for peace and understanding can seem naïve and inappropriate, especially to those who suffer the immediate pain or loss and the shock of being attacked. And yet, as I hope to show, in the wake of suffering it is essential that we do call for those things, because the peace we demand can be *our* peace, and the understanding that we want can provide *us* with a way of dealing with the horror. Buddhism, I believe, can offer comfort and hope, and open up a space for us to try to understand if not *why* such terrible things occur then *how* we might best respond to them. By comprehending how we suffer individually and collectively, we can better appreciate how interrelated our world is and therefore how best to work together to solve its problems.

1 ❈ Impermanence

For Siddhartha Gautama, the Buddha, the nature of suffering was the essential question facing all human beings. It was something that afflicted rich or poor, the powerful or the powerless, men or women. How the Buddha came to understand this is the foundational story of the Buddhist religion.

As a young man, the Buddha lived in luxury as a prince of the realm, confined by his father Suddhodana in a palace in northern India and surrounded by numerous riches and pleasurable diversions. One day, however, while riding in his coach through the city, he glanced out of the window and saw an old man, hunched over, leaning on a cane, making his way home. Questioning his driver as to what was wrong with the man, the young prince was told that the man was merely old, a condition that comes to us all. On another day, the prince saw a man who appeared very sick, and, on asking what he saw, was told by his driver that the individual was indeed sick and that we too are all subject to sickness. On yet another journey, the young man saw a dead body, and the driver reminded him that we all die. Finally, the Buddha saw a man robed in yellow with no hair on his head and was told this was a *sanyasin*, an ascetic, who had renounced the wealth of the world and wandered through it seeking serenity.

The young man went home to the palace. Then, leaving behind his wife and child and ceding them all his possessions, he shaved his head, and became a *sanyasin*. He visited many teachers and practiced many disciplines, including extreme asceticism. Finding that such asceticism had not brought him to the Truth, the renunciate rested underneath a bodhi tree and, sitting cross-legged, decided that he would not get up until he had achieved Enlightenment. After being tormented by the demon, Mara—who attempted to distract him with false hopes and desires—Siddhartha Gautama achieved enlightenment, and became the Enlightened One, or Buddha.

The consequences of the Buddha's enlightenment were his realization of the Four Noble Truths. Theses truths form the core of Buddhist teachings. They are, first, that all existence is suffering; secondly, that this suffering has a cause; thirdly, that suffering can be overcome; and, fourthly, that there is a way to bring about the end of suffering. Contemplating how to bring about release from suffering, the Buddha realized the Eightfold Path. These principles are: right understanding, right thought, right speech, right action, right livelihood, right effort, right mindfulness, and right concentration. In sum, these principles are as follows: Once we understand the causes of suffering and cultivate action based on correct thinking and thoughtful speech, if we also live correctly and with mindfulness and practice meditation, then the path is open to overcome the suffering inherent in being alive.

Buddhism, therefore, is a very practical religion. It is concerned with finding solutions to pressing needs. Already as a young man in his coach, the Buddha saw how our life is full of suffering—sickness, old age, and death—and he was shocked by it. What the wealthy, sheltered, perhaps almost willfully naïve young man realized is that these central events in our life were no longer abstractions or the experience of only the poor; they were inevitable and came to everyone, even this wealthy, handsome prince, who had it all. The central purpose of the Buddha's life then became trying to find a way to understand and then overcome suffering.

When something terrible happens we tend to ask the same questions: Why did it have to happen? Why did so many good people have to die, and die so horribly? Where was God? What should be the correct response? How can we stop this happening again? How do we grieve? How do we move on?

Beyond the practical answers of providing succor and help, shipping in medical or food supplies, mobilizing emergency services, considering the best means to respond politically or developmentally, offering financial or personal support, these questions point to larger, more metaphysical issues that require a more internal reckoning, one starker and perhaps more difficult to contemplate. For, if there is one thing that terrible events such as earthquakes or tsunamis, plane crashes or building collapses, fires or bombings prove, it is that everything is impermanent. That a place or a group of people could be present in one moment and then destroyed by a wave or be a mass of smoke and human debris the next teaches us better than any *sutra*, or religious saying, that our lives are desperately fragile. Even the strongest structure or the fittest and most capable individual cannot escape impermanence.

Impermanence is the direct consequence of the fact that humans, like all things, are conditioned: We come into being, we stay for a while and flourish, we decay or vanish, and the cycle starts again. As the Mahanirvana Sutra states: "All phenomena and matter are subject to impermanence." This truth is of fundamental importance in understanding Buddhism's view of the world. So important is it that the Buddha's last words are reported to have been on this very matter: "Subject to change are all things, strive on with diligence."

When people unfamiliar with Buddhist teachings think of impermanence, they tend to think such a doctrine is very pessimistic—everything and everyone fades and dies, nothing and no one lasts. However, I believe that the concept is neither pessimistic nor optimistic; it is simply realistic. The Buddha discerned it with the old man, the sick individual, and the dead body: they had once been young, healthy, and alive like him. And we don't have to be the man who became the Buddha to see these things. The real world constantly reveals to us that change is constant, and change doesn't always happen in ways that match our perceptions or internal desires. I'm sure a thousand examples come to your mind: a friend who practices a healthy lifestyle suddenly dies in a car crash or gets cancer; the partner of a relative who's just married and looks forward to a long life passes away from a heart attack; the young man who promised so much dies of leukemia or comes down with schizophrenia or becomes addicted to drugs; the job we like at the company we care about vanishes as the business files for bankruptcy; the house we buy springs a leak and its walls crack.

What the Buddha realized is that it is through clinging to the idea of permanence that suffering occurs. By attaching ourselves to permanence and filling it full of values of worth and goodness, we make the inevitable changes that our life undergoes painful. By not always keeping in mind the inevitability of mutability, we're always surprised and challenged by that change, and this leads to suffering.

For most of us, impermanence is a terrifying concept. Because of impermanence, good things go bad. Our possessions break or stop working. We lose our livelihoods. We die. Impermanence does not appear a good thing. Consequently, we all desire its opposite. When I was young, I hoped I'd look more mature than my years. Now that I am nearly fifty, however, I don't want people to remind me of how old I am! Like many of us, I'd like to be young forever. I don't want to face having to grow old. Permanence is deeply desirable.

This view of impermanence, however, depends on understanding the self as a defined, absolute identity. For those of us in the West, obsessed as we are with the concept of self, the radicalism of Buddhism's observation on impermanence is what makes Buddhism so challenging. We believe we are absolute entities; we are proud of our personalities; we identify with them and refuse to change. But we *can* change. We *can* get better, move on, try again. This is also a condition of impermanence—that we can be free to change, attempt to correct the former mistakes we've made, challenge ourselves to throw off the shackles of fate or poor health and economic disadvantage and change them all for the better. After all, if we couldn't do this, what would be the point of education? We should remember that the Buddha in his last words not only recognized impermanence but he also exhorted his followers to "strive on with diligence." Recognizing impermanence doesn't mean that we shouldn't achieve anything, or that change only happens for the worse. This is another essential lesson of Buddhism. I will talk about the personal sense of impermanence later on in the book.

I realize that always keeping in mind the fact that everything is impermanent isn't easy to do. Yet if we carry in our minds the idea that everything is going to change—that even though we may live with someone for sixty, seventy, even eighty years, our loved ones or we ourselves will die, or that they and we may perhaps go in an instant—then that change becomes a little easier to tolerate. Furthermore, the very transience of life and its vulnerability, the knowledge that the world is fragile and delicate, can help us cherish the moments when we are together with our loved ones and honor and enjoy the short number of years we are allotted in each lifetime.

Indeed, the death of something can bring about the birth of something else. It is a fundamental law of the natural world that the decomposition of matter allows other things to grow and develop. When a forest burns, there is not only the regeneration of new life, but sometimes it emerges in even greater profusion and variety. Some forests even require fire for their regeneration. When an animal dies in the ecosystem, other animals feed on, and life forms grow out of, the dead body. In this way, the world is kept fresh and recharged. This doctrine of impermanence also offers hope to everyone living under tyranny or oppression. Even the most despotic of tyrants will die; even the greatest of empires will inevitably come to an end; even the most intractable and irreducible of problems can be changed over time. The world is littered with the remnants of enormous statues to the powerful rulers of past ages that have crumbled or have been dispersed by the winds or washed away by the tide.

The recognition of the neutrality of impermanence—an understanding that death is neither good nor bad, but merely a fact—is one of Buddhism's great gifts. It helps us grasp that the reason why we are afraid of death and suffering is not because they're too present to us but, to the contrary, because, in our fear, we refuse to admit they're with us. Paradoxically, only by grasping on to suffering and death will we be given the insight and wisdom that will help us recover a degree of equanimity.

2 ❋ Karma

While natural disasters, freak accidents, bombings, robberies, illness, and other calamities show how vulnerable the world we live in can be, we shouldn't believe that the world is governed only by randomness or chaos. Impermanence doesn't mean complete unpredictability. There are causes and conditions, and causes and conditions in the past lead to results in the present moment. If we want to know what the causes of our present condition are then we have to look at the results and traumas of our life in the past. In addition, if we want to know what will happen in the future, then we need to look at our actions at this moment.

When Buddhism talks about cause and effect, there is a tendency to think that Buddhism is, in effect, blaming the victim because of what he or she may have done in a past life and exonerating the perpetrator for the same reason. This is

a simplistic notion that perverts the deeper meaning of cause
and effect and karma.

Buddhists believe that understanding cause and effect
demands that we attempt to see the whole picture and not
just isolate the causes and effects of our actions that are con-
venient for us. Buddhism asks us to look at the world honestly, and not just as our politicians, parents, society, or our
own fears tell us to do. The laws of cause and effect are ruth-
less and unstoppable—both for good and ill—and they need
to be grasped very well if the negative is to be minimized
and the positive maximized. The laws cannot be eradicated;
the actions one undertakes cannot vanish. When the causes
and conditions come together then we have to face the effects. So it is incumbent on us to create healthy outcomes
by setting up the causes for healthy outcomes, to minimize
the possibility for negative results, and to develop global cit-
izens who are honest, thoughtful, and compassionate by not
only creating the environment for honesty, thoughtfulness,
and compassion to flourish but by being honest, thoughtful,
and compassionate ourselves.

The laws of cause and effect don't operate as baldly as
the previous sentence might suggest. Indeed, they can be subtle and profound, mysterious and inscrutable. Nor do I mean
to suggest that everyone's actions are predetermined and that
we don't have free will to decide how we will react to any
given situation. We see this clearly when a catastrophic event
happens. Some people behave badly: they loot, they profiteer,

or they may use the situation to stir up hatred and consolidate power. Some people behave well. They drop everything they're doing and rush to rescue people; they set up food pantries and clothing drives and homeless shelters; they take in the orphaned or the bereaved; they send money; they help clean up and rebuild. Some use the opportunity of mutual suffering to put aside age-old differences and forge new relationships. At times like these, we also tend to discover that what is truly valuable in life is not material possessions or having a lot of money. Instead, we rediscover community and courage and working for something greater than our personal safety. We also have the opportunity to see how attached we have been to trivialities and things that ultimately have no value. As you can see, therefore, terrible events give us an opportunity to respond positively or negatively, to reflect on our choices and bring about change for the better.

Of course, there are countless tragic events happening throughout the world at any one time, and we cannot respond to all of them. It is also true that some of them occur beyond the attention of the global media and many millions of people suffer without the larger international community responding. But it would be wrong to think that because they seem to happen in isolation they don't have an effect. There are no such things as isolated tragedies. They all have a cause and they all lead to an effect, whether these are as practical as movements of large numbers of people or pressure on food or water supplies, or as intangible as an increasing sense of helplessness among individuals that makes them less able to resist the next calamity to come along or causes them to be incapable of furthering their personal and collective goals.

The challenge of Buddhism, therefore, is to extend compassion as broadly as possible and recognize the inter-connections of cause and effect within all suffering: that suffering everywhere is our suffering; and that our suffering is the world's. To use a medical analogy, simply cutting out the infected area or severing the infected body part will not solve the problem. When we have compassion, we see the infection from the perspective of the whole body. The infection is not merely localized; it is a part of the body that is diseased. Consequently, the whole body needs to be healed rather than us simply cutting out the offending section.

The connections of cause and effect through time thus require a holistic response that pays attention to history—and not merely our own. It means acknowledging the larger body that is the human family. It means recognizing that we can neither engage with nor flee from the world without consequence. We are *all* connected.

The laws of cause and effect act through time to make every action haunt or support us in the future. Buddhism's re-lationality—its sense that everything is dependent—stands in opposition to the doctrines of isolation and self-containment that many people in the West feel is the normal state of being. In the United States, we like to have privacy—one based on the central role of private property and individual liberty as

the governing ideas of the laws of the country. But, sometimes, that sense of the need to defend one's own becomes
non-communication and ignorance. We don't like to know
what goes on elsewhere: we stay in our nice neighborhoods
and don't go to the ghettos or poor areas. Understandably
perhaps, we want to protect ourselves.

Self-protection, however, is not enough. We can never
fully isolate ourselves, never escape from dependence. Buddhism teaches us to recognize our interdependence and then
instructs us on taking responsibility not only for ourselves
but for the whole society. What happens in ghettos and poor
countries impacts us by making us fearful. Our lives, therefore, are conditioned by fear in the same way they would be
if we drove through a neighborhood and were worried about
being shot. Fear is fear, whatever the probability of its being
justified.

Buddhism's concern is not simply with our individual
lives or of those who live around us. It is not limited by the
desires of the nation state or of geopolitical regions. Indeed,
Buddhism is not content to rest at this planet. As a sutra says,
a thousand solar systems make up the extent of a small world;
a thousand small worlds make up the extent of an
intermediate world; and a thousand middle worlds make up
the extent of the big world. This is what is meant in Buddhism by the "three layers of the thousand worlds." In this
way, Buddhism seeks to convey its belief that there are unlimited worlds in the universe, each of them exerting an influ-

ence on our individual lives and each of our individual lives exerting an influence on the innumerable universes.

If we perceive existence in such a way, it can only teach us to be both humble and awesomely aware of our responsibility. Buddhism argues that everything we do has a consequence. Whether the cause is good or bad, whether it is in thought or deed, it always leads to an effect. Sometimes, the action is relatively inconsequential: if I knock into the table, I feel pain. Why? Because when I exert force upon the table there is a reaction against my hand and it hurts. This is the consequence, a punishment, if you will, for my initial action. In a similar way, a car moves because the energy it releases creates thrust that pushes the car forward. To paraphrase the maxim from physics: Every reaction has an equal, if not always opposite, reaction. But, simultaneously, we are a tiny presence in the huge pushes and pulls of cause and effect throughout the universe and that should encourage humility.

By looking at things holistically, by placing oneself in the shoes of another, one has the opportunity to grasp the spatial dimension of cause and effect and act more prudently to maximize the good and minimize the bad consequences of one's actions. The world did it in the aftermath of World War II in Western Europe, where broken societies were given the money and the resources to move from being seedbeds of dictatorship to gardens of democracy; the United States did the same in Japan. But it takes time, patience, and persistence. At every moment, we have an opportunity to replace the old divisions and longstanding grievances and subsequent outrages that characterize our world with a different set of causes and effects. We can do it on an individual level: with our family and friends, with our neighbors, in our community, in our cities and states, and in our country, and then beyond. In so doing we increase the sum of good, which then extends outwards, affecting everything positively until it can encompass the universe.

We also need to rethink the idea that we are independent beings. We like to think we are self-sufficient, self-determined, and self-motivating. We believe that we are entitled to certain things, that we deserve what we want because we are self-contained. But we all have to live and work together. Simply to get through life requires cooperation and mutual interdependence. When we are babies, we are utterly dependent upon others for our clothing, our food, our shelter, and our protection. Our dependence on others continues throughout our life. Our physical body and feelings depend on our contact with the outside world, a world where our memory and experience also interact. From the interpersonal to the international, we all rely on one another to help us achieve what we strive for. Shops need us to buy products from them; countries require other countries to trade with; we need someone else to form a family. If we can truly realize this—in our individual and communal lives, and between the nations—then the suffering to which we are all subject will be diminished.

We have seen how Buddhism argues that we are all interconnected and live interdependently and that everything has a cause and effect. The question that now poses itself is: What is the factor that binds us together and reveals our interconnectedness? Buddhists understand this phenomenon through the concept of *karma*. As we all live interdependently or interconnectedly, we share the results from the collective karma. Whatever our feelings about a calamitous event or a personal tragedy, there is some sort of karmic connection, whether collective or individual. Indirectly or directly, we are all affected.

The concept of karma is hard for any of us to take—especially if, like so many of us, we are wrapped up in the pain of loss and seeking for some understanding of why tragedy happens to us, or how we can bring perpetrators of crimes to justice. Buddhism may at times like these seem a little unyielding in its honest attempt to respond to the hardest experiences of our life. Yet, I believe that a true understanding of karma offers a way forward for justice as well as healing.

The word *karma* literally means "act" or "volition." Karma always has a cause and it always has an effect, and it has three aspects: the thought processes that lead you to the act; the carrying out of the act; and how you talk about it. I remember once seeing an advertisement on TV that had the tagline, "Whatever the path you walk through, you will always leave a trace." This touches on the meaning on karma, except that I always say that it is not only the path you walk through that bears your imprint; even *thinking* or *talking* about the path leaves some trace, some energy. After all, in order to do anything, we need to have the idea in our mind. These thoughts accumulate mental karma and lead us to the place where physical karma is acted out.

Now, I should be clear that, by suggesting that all actions are in some way premeditated, I'm not saying that people who suffer and die in accidents are karmically drawn to their deaths, and that they were directly responsible for their own deaths. What Buddhism teaches is that it's important to look at any incident as not just an isolated, single happening. Buddhism asks us to expand time and space and follow causes and effects. Sometimes, as I've indicated already, that process can be mysterious and baffling.

The ultimate question we always ask ourselves when confronted by tragedy remains a great mystery: "Why did good people have to die in such a terrible way?" Some might say that karma in some way absolves perpetrators from their acts of harm because it makes all of us somehow involved— we all like to believe that we can get away with something if we can. According to Buddhism, however, if you do something good or bad, there is *always* a reaction. This will be recorded as your karma or karmic force. So we have to be aware of what we are saying or thinking because this karmic force will accumulate in our consciousness and carry over in our reincarnation or rebirth. In this way, Buddhism, although it talks of the impermanence of the self, is not about absolving individuals from their actions. Far from it! Because we are interdependent, all our actions have consequences. Buddhism, therefore, teaches the utmost respect for others, precisely because we *are* those others. Consequently, the serial killer who gets away with his murders will receive punishment in a future lifetime through the karma he accumulated in this one; the kind and compassionate individual who dies young will receive rewards in a future lifetime through the same process.

I don't underestimate for a moment how hard this is to stomach. It goes against all our gut beliefs in immediate retribution against those who commit harm and for immediate reward for those who are virtuous. But all the world's major religions have sought to address this conundrum of how the good die young or the evil go unpunished in this lifetime, and provide a degree of comfort to the afflicted by positing a situation after death where the injustices of this world are in some way balanced. I once met a man who told me he didn't believe in life after death. He thought the physical body simply faded away, leaving nothing behind. I asked him whether he believed in justice and universal truth. What, I asked, if a serial killer, who had killed and robbed a lot of people, got away from the law, led a long life, and died peacefully, unpunished for his crime? Would you be willing to accept this, I asked the man? He didn't have an answer, but I believe even he wouldn't have accepted the answer that good goes unrewarded and evil goes unpunished in the universe.

Buddhism also believes in life after death. However, it doesn't consider the consignment to heaven or hell of an individual the end of that person's life, or indeed of that individual's responsibility for his or her actions. *Samsara*, or the cycle of birth–death–rebirth, continues through eons, and it doesn't affect only humans, but all sentient beings. Karma adds to the mystery of a person's passing by positing that, although it may seem shocking that some people survive disasters while others perish, we don't know the karmic reasons why they had to die, since karma operates throughout time—into the past, within the present, and into the future. Moreover, karma functions like a plant. A plant can blossom once a year, or may live for only two years, or every year. Each plant blossoms at different times and under different conditions; plants that seem dead may spring to life while others may bloom at the point of death. People who do bad things in this life may not receive retribution in this life, but will experience suffering in the next or the one after that, etc. People who do good things may suffer because of what they did in previous lives.

Just as the laws of cause and effect are immutable, so is the natural law of justice. Good deeds will create good karma; bad deeds bad karma. Justice will always be served in the end. Even terrible situations may not be the coming to fruition of bad karma, but instead the ripening of good karma, a mobilization for compassion and justice, a concerted effort to root out the causes of the suffering. Thus, out of great evil could come great good. What we must protect against, however, is creating unintended victims of our karmic actions. We are all potential or actual victims and we are all potential or actual perpetrators. Buddhism's challenge is to turn bad karma into good, and not to add to bad karma out of fear or anger or a need to exact revenge.

3 ✽ Justice

In my last chapter I mentioned the desire we have to bring about justice when bad things happen. We want the innocent to be given their chance to see the guilty punished for what they've done. If, as I say, Buddhism operates over great stretches of time, then what does it mean to bring someone to justice? Is not this simply complacency and fatalism to sit back and wait for the laws of the universe to bring an individual to justice for what they've done?

Justice is a function of natural law, and, like karma, works both in the past, present, and the future. In the Buddhist context, neither a divinity nor the Buddha himself passes judgment on us or punishes us. It is our own karma that will perform that function. Put simply, if an action comes from good intentions then there will be a good reaction. If the action comes from bad intentions then there will be a bad reaction. The universe acts as justice itself, and the universe is never compromised. For instance, if we damage the Earth's ecosystems, we will suffer the consequences. Some people may get rich in the process, but their descendants will suffer as a result of what they have done. In this regard, the operation of the world is the operation of justice. It is not a function of human justice, because human justice is conditioned. This is why justice needs to be thought of as separate from punishment. Punishment as justice merely perpetuates a cycle of more punishment as justice. But true justice is not about punishment; it is about being aware of cause and effect.

Justice is absolutely impartial—it is merely the sum of good and bad actions operating within the universe. However, we can model human laws so that more good is generated than bad. This is why one of the principle ideas of Buddhism is nonviolence. Nonviolence means not doing anything to make bad situations worse as well as not creating bad situations. By creating conditions that enhance the possibility of performing good deeds, rather than simply creating laws to stop people doing bad things, we create situations where less violence is needed because there are fewer situations where violence is generated. Justice in this situation, therefore, is prospective rather than retrospective. We create a just situation *before* the crime has been committed, because we make it less likely that a crime *will* be committed.

This wisdom is also hard for people to understand, because they tend not to think there is any need for justice before a crime has been committed. They do not think of injustice being a cause of suffering before anyone has done anything wrong. If poverty leads many people to rob banks, sell drugs, loot, or behave pathologically, then why not address poverty rather than wait for people to become sociopaths and then lock them up and complain about how destructive they are? If a poor education or a lack of viable work options or a collective despair in a community lead young men to commit murder and end up on death row, costing the taxpayers a lot of money and tying up the criminal justice system, why is it not justice to turn schools into places of excellence, find meaningful work for the graduates of those schools, and cultivate optimism and enthusiasm for life? All the evidence suggests that it is more efficacious and better for society to prevent crime in the first place than to spend much more time, energy, and money attempting to clean up the mess afterward. It would also reduce the injustices after the crime, simply because fewer crimes will have been committed.

Consider the effects of the tsunami in 2004 and Hurricane Katrina in 2005. The effects of both tragedies were enhanced because, in the first case, wetlands that lined the shoreline and could have absorbed the storm surge had been cut down, and, in the second, because people were living below sea level and the levees that held back the waters had not been reinforced. Preserving the wetlands, allowing them to remain undeveloped to absorb rising tides, and keeping levees repaired were specific preventive measures that would have saved many people's lives and reduced suffering. It would also have be an important aspect of justice. Now that climate change has been accepted as a scientific fact, we have the option to act in advance of even greater environmental disasters to make sure that justice is served by misery and suffering being prevented.

Of course, karmic laws are complicated and life is never easy, and our choices are not always so clearly made. We have constantly to weigh the options between actions, always bearing in mind the need to foster the good and to limit the bad. This is why laws should be created to nurture the well-being of humans. Unfortunately, some people have made laws to punish or destroy other human beings rather than bring about justice and I think this is opposite to the intent of natural law. The law should help people by removing the conditions for suffering and negative actions and create the conditions for justice. But we all get caught up in legalism, bureaucracy, the need for revenge and the hope that if we just move something or someone out of sight the problem will go away.

So, as you can see, like our response to suffering, the application of justice needs to be looked at holistically. We need to try to see the situation from many angles before we make judgments. Only this way can we make sense of why someone can kill another person and yet not be punished for it in this lifetime. Buddhists know that that person will pay a heavy karmic debt in future lifetimes. Furthermore, we can seek to understand the wrongdoer's action by looking at the conditions that led him to kill another person, and thereby not only provide an apt punishment for the individual, but also make sure that such conditions are not ripe for more people to do the same thing in the future.

A question that might be asked at this point is how we should make judgments about what is wrong. How do we bring people who do bad things to justice? Indeed, what is justice when everything is conditioned? Buddhism acknowledges that we have a mind and that the mind makes judgments. Judgments in and of themselves are not necessarily inherently bad or good. Like all actions, they have a cause and effect, and thus can create good or bad causes and effects. Now, clearly, judgment is necessary for our survival. We tell children not to touch fire because they'll be burned, or we tell them not to go swimming in deep water because they could drown, or they shouldn't eat dog food because it is not meant for human beings. In these circumstances, we clearly have a prior idea that leads us to make the judgment that is based on our knowledge of the effect that putting your hand in a fire might have and that the child is ignorant of it. We project an effect into the future because we understand the cause of harm.

But these judgments, while sensible, are still conditioned, a result of some form of experience or cultural understanding. There's nothing inherent in these judgments that separates them from a conclusion, for instance, that black people are criminals or people with yellow skins are materialistic, or women are weak. These are prejudices that also depend on our projections. As such, therefore, the judgments are conditioned by our cultural background (which might be sheltered or blinkered), our family's mores (which may be narrow or undisciplined), our sense of ourselves (which may be over-inflated or negative), our experiences (which may be limited or particular), and intuitive reactions (which may be based on fear or disgust).

Buddhism holds that all people are the same in that we are all conditioned, interdependent beings, no matter what our gender, color, religion, sexual orientation, or state of mind. During the course of our lives we are exposed to different conditions, all of which have causes and all of which have consequences. So we need to be careful that our loving care for protecting our children and telling them to watch out for strangers doesn't merge with our cultural conditioning that they should watch out for strangers with different-colored skin or different religious views. More facts or knowledge may not guarantee that we become aware of our conditioning. Only wisdom can do that.

Thus justice means recognizing our prejudices and understanding our self-serving motivations and working for the benefit of all beings. This is a great challenge. Nonetheless, if we are to stop violence and perpetuate peace, we must set ourselves the hard tasks. It also means that when we bring perpetrators to justice, and it is right that we aim to do so, we act judiciously and thoughtfully, and see it is an opportunity not only to make sure that the punishment is commensurate with the crime, but that, more challengingly, it leads to an outcome whereby all of society is encouraged to pursue the good rather than forced to wall itself even more against the bad. Otherwise, justice itself is not well served.

4 ❈ Faith

After September 11, many people found themselves looking at how faith contributes to suffering. Indeed, when one thinks of the violence that has occurred throughout human history, much of it can be categorized as a result of a struggle of one religion to assert itself over another or of individuals using their religion as a pretext for earthly power or material enrichment. Yet religion is merely the path that helps us to explore the truth within. It is, in essence, a means to an end. Nevertheless, throughout history to the present, countless people have viewed religion not as a sacred path to the truth, but Truth itself. And yet, no one religion can be equated with Truth or the Ultimate. Each of the world's major religions has a history, a timespan; but Truth cannot have a timespan, and, by definition, it cannot be conditional or temporally bound.

The truths that religions seek and espouse are eternal, but the religions themselves are historically fixed in time.

As a Zen parable describes it, the master or teacher instructs by pointing the finger to the moon. To cling to one's own belief as Truth itself—or even as the sole means to Truth—is like clinging to the master's finger only, without seeing the moon at all. However, even the moon itself is not to be equated with Truth. The Ultimate is perceived only when we make the mind as clean as a mirror, to reflect the moon and all its surroundings within it. To clean this mirror-like surface, we need to remove the murky illusion of self that divides our world, to lift ourselves out of the categories with which we frame our lives. An example of this is in the Diamond Sutra, where the Buddha tells his disciples, "My teaching is like the raft you shall abandon after you cross the river. You shall not carry it on the shoulders after you get on the shore." In other words, religion is a tool to reach enlightenment; after enlightenment or true wisdom is reached, religion is no longer necessary.

Communication and dialogue among members of differing religious frameworks are major steps toward the overcoming of artificial boundaries, the removal of illusions and prejudices within us, and the search for common ground and universal truths between us. In short, we need to respect each other's faiths and learn from them. For instance, when he prayed for the victims of September 11, respecting all their faiths, Venerable Master Hsing Yun, began his prayer with:

"Buddha, God, Jesus. . . ." He believes it is possible to have more than one belief. Indeed, religious pluralism can help us avoid the kind of blind faith that misleads some people to such an extent that they destroy other lives along with their own and believe they will go to heaven.

I do not mean, however, to suggest that we destroy the boundaries and differences that distinguish our various traditions and religious beliefs. Rather, it is hoped that we might seek a way to transcend such categories in search of common truths, to remain confident that no truth can call itself the name if it fears being questioned or challenged. On the contrary, the greatest truths are found through constant seeking and persistent inquiry. They are born out of mystery and should be approached with humility. Seeking and inquiring the truths of other faiths doesn't mean we turn our backs even for a moment on our own unique religions—just as seeking transcendent truths should never mean one stops working among all people of the world to better their conditions. As one who has been engaged with interreligious dialogue for several years, I can attest to the fact that learning about other faiths has only deepened my own convictions and brought me greater understanding of Buddhism. I have talked with people of other faiths who feel the same way. All of us need to transcend our everyday categories—not to abandon them, but to discover higher truths, greater beauty, and apply this knowledge to our everyday world. It is a work of vital importance if we are to reduce the suffering caused by those who believe in the absolutism of their faith and wish to impose it by force on others.

When one realizes that the self and the various categories it creates, including religion itself, are, in a sense, merely arbitrary boundaries that can be transcended, one begins to see the world as a far more hopeful place. Fundamentally, we are all united—Christians, Muslims, Hindus, Jews, and Buddhists alike. To heal ourselves we must transcend our differences, and atone for our prejudices—for to *atone* is to be *at one*. In fact, we need to consider the possibility that unless we do transcend religion as a category, we cannot truly hope to practice the ideals that religion professes to embody. When we look at the world today, the perils of thinking only in terms of the superiority of our own religious tradition become very clear.

5 ❋ Death and Evil

Because Buddhism doesn't believe that death is the end of the story, it paradoxically offers a corrective to the idea that death itself doesn't matter. Death is the great balancer: it falls upon men and women, the rich and the poor, the benevolent and the malevolent alike. Death stops greed and it curtails poverty; it measures life and, in Buddhist terms, initiates birth. It is finite and yet infinite.

How we die is a very important aspect of Buddhist thinking and practice. Buddhism demands that we pay great attention to how our mind is throughout life so that, when we die, we experience peace and can detach ourselves from our body with equanimity. It does this from the perspective that, even though it may feel as though we are in hell, the actual moment of dying is only a short experience in the span of our many lives.

Buddhism suggests there are six realms that govern existence. The lowest realm—or the realm that is most affected by bad karmic conditions—is the region of hell. The next lowest is that of ghosts or spirits. The realm karmically above the realm of ghosts is that of the animals. The next realm is that of the Asuras, or titanic gods or demons, followed by that of human beings. The final realm is that of heaven, or the realm of the gods. Unlike Judaism and Christianity, which see heaven and hell as utterly separate dimensions, Buddhism believes that an individual goes through all of these dimensions depending on his or her karmic history. So, for Buddhism, neither heaven nor hell is necessarily your ultimate dimension. Indeed, heaven is not necessarily the place you end up when you are completely good and hell where you end up when you have been irredeemably bad. In heaven, for instance, it is possible to experience a surfeit of wealth and joy and become so lax in the continued cultivation of wisdom—the ultimate aim of all Buddhists—that you are incarnated in a lower realm.

Buddhism venerates individuals who work their many lives seeking to remove the causes of suffering and karma through their presence and actions so that all beings may be released from suffering. They are called *bodhisattvas*, and they vow to help individuals, both human and non-human, not only on earth and in heaven, but also in hell. Most people who are reborn in the hell realm are there because of the accumulation of bad karma. However, there are some beings that are reborn in hell because that is their vow. One such being is the Ksitigarbha bodhisattva, who vows to save all the sentient beings in hell.

This conception of hell is one that is puzzling not just to monotheists. There is the story of a disciple who came to his Zen (or Chan in Chinese) master with a question: "Master, after you die, where are you going to be reborn?"

"In hell," the Master replied.

The disciple was confused. "Why would someone as spiritually refined and cultivated as yourself be reborn in hell?"

"If I am not reborn in hell," the Master replied, "then who is going to save you?"

This conception of existence means that at any moment we are surrounded by those on their way to hell and those on their way to heaven and, most importantly, by bodhisattvas who are working all the time to enable us to change our lives for the better. What we need to understand is that we can individually make a hell of heaven and a heaven of hell through our actions. Furthermore, by not attaching ego to the actions and not concentrating on the effects of our good deeds, we can make a difference.

Bodhisattvas make a vow to save all sentient beings, no matter how infinite in number, before they attain the ultimate goal, which is *nirvana* or the removal from the cycle of samsara altogether. The broadness of the vow and the impossibility of its fulfillment are intrinsically bound up with each other, and show both the essence and the ultimate expression of what Buddhism means by compassion. It is not merely one's family or friends, or even one's countrymen and—women who are to be extended infinite compassion. It is not even only humans. It is all sentient beings. I have a friend who is the founder of an animal protectionist organization. One day, recalling the bodhisattva pledge, he said to me, "Yifa, I vow to save all the sentient beings in the world."

"That's good you've vowed to do that," I told him. "But don't expect it to happen."

"Why?" he asked.

"Because," I replied, "animals, just like human beings, are unlimited. Their suffering is endless."

But my animal protection friend is not going to change, and nor should he. Animals are suffering in huge numbers in slaughterhouses and factory farms, in laboratories and on fur farms, in junkyards or in fighting pits throughout the world. They, too, deserve to have their suffering recognized and someone to care for them. Like a good bodhisattva, my animal protectionist friend will keep working to stop the suffering of all sentient beings, no matter how endless the suffering or how numerous the sentient beings are.

Doctors also act as bodhisattvas. On one of my regular visits to my doctor I said to him: "You are very good, but you never run out of patients. Even the ones you have cured come back to you again. Do you ever expect to finish healing all the patients in the world?" His answer, of course, was that he didn't. I know the doctor turns up each morning ready to try to cure those patients lined up outside his office. His vow to use his skills to help the suffering is another example of a bodhisattva in action.

When many of us are confronted with the suffering of the world we are overwhelmed. Even as a Buddhist nun I often feel swamped by that wave of misery. We wonder what we can do. We feel paralyzed. When I was talking with the animal advocate and the doctor, I wasn't arguing that they should stop trying to alleviate suffering. Far from it: Buddhists make it our central goal. What I meant, however, is that we should go about alleviating suffering with humility and without attachment. Attachment here doesn't mean a lack of interest or some sort of indifference. What it means is that we shouldn't attach ego or pride or greed to the action. We should recognize that suffering is endless, and *still* go about doing all we can to lessen it.

There is a famous story attributed to the writer Loren Eiseley that explains what I mean. The story goes that a man was walking along the seashore one day. On the sand he saw countless starfish, thousands upon thousands of them, which had been carried by the tide onto the beach and were dying in the heat of the sun. The man felt helpless at seeing all these bodies piling up. Then he saw a girl picking starfish up and one by one throwing them back into the sea. The man went up to the child and asked her what she was doing?

"I'm rescuing the starfish," said the girl.

"But there are thousands and thousands of them," said the man. "Do you think what you're doing is going to make a difference?"

The girl looked at him and pointed to the starfish in her hand. "It makes a difference to *this* starfish," she said.

This story illuminates a central truth in Buddhism. Without hope for reward and, in some way, acknowledging the hopelessness of her task, the child yet felt compassion for each individual sentient being she came across. She did not see life as a collective, and nor was she overwhelmed and paralyzed by the enormous suffering taking place on the beach. Instead, she focused on what she *could* do and saved those individuals she *could* save, because she knew that each of the starfish lives mattered to each individual starfish, and that in the end was what counted. Likewise, the Buddhist, as a bodhisattva, takes on the task of rescuing all sentient beings and postponing his or her own liberation from the cycle of death–birth–rebirth, so that, in his or her own particular way, he or she can throw individual starfish back into the water.

There is an additional component that needs to be understood here, and that is that those isolated starfish are in some way connected to you. Thus, in saving the starfish you save yourself and everything all at the same time. There is a well-known saying in Buddhism: "From one flower you can see the whole world." Although the flower opens up in one moment, yet it did not just suddenly bloom. The sun, the rain, the soil, and the bees nurtured it. It too came from a seed, or a root, or a tuber that in turn came from seeds, roots, or tubers. That flower contains in it the sum of the past growth and decay of its forebears and it contains the germ of future seeds for generations to come. If we are to take any action on behalf of anything, we need to acknowledge that. What we eat, what we wear, what materials we consume—all were made or grown using natural resources by other individuals, transported by other individuals, transformed by chemicals or manufacturing by other individuals. Everything we have created, everything we are, is the sum of an infinite number of other acts. To honor the flower, to honor the details, is to honor everything—to bring into the hell of lives a little bit of heaven.

In the West, when we see bad things happen, we often use the notion of evil as a way to explain what happened. Either the individual who carried out the acts or the deed itself is evil. In Buddhism, evil is in essence bad karma, and since everything is conditioned, evil is not a static, indescribable presence—as it sometimes seems in Christianity—but conditioned.

I like to think of evil in terms of water and wind. When there is no wind, water in a pond is still. However, when there is wind, the pond produces waves. But waves are not separate entities from the water; they are made of the same substance. It is only the conditioned activity of wind that turns the water from motionlessness to movement. In the same way, evil (and for that matter, good) is merely a transfer in the nature of the condition, from stillness to movement. Because of this, bodhisattvas can retrieve even the worst offenders, even after their deaths. Likewise, everyone has the opportunity to become a Buddha, or "enlightened one." Everyone has a Buddha nature.

I often liken evil to fertilizer. It may stink and not be pleasant to be around, but it can allow good things to grow. The Buddha once said, "defilement is enlightenment; enlightenment is defilement." What he meant was not that we should cultivate desire—whether for money, power, sex, or the host of other things that we want to take for ourselves. Rather he meant that we should make attempts to become aware of the desire so we can encounter and analyze it better. The Buddha knew that we shouldn't be afraid of desire, because we need to be able to see through it and observe its emptiness. This is why I believe it's better to bring the garbage into the open where we can deal with it rather than keep it piling up in the basement. We need to be honest about the source of that evil and confront our role in allowing it to occur.

For Buddhists, the nature of the condition of good and evil is also called emptiness. There is no such thing as "the wave." The wave is the condition of water. There is no such thing as "the wind." The wind is the condition of air. There is no such thing as "water." Water is the condition of hydrogen and oxygen. There is no such thing as "air." Air is the condition of hydrogen, oxygen, nitrogen, and other gasses. These elements are, in turn, made of molecules. These molecules are made of electrons and neutrons, and these in turn of sub-atomic particles that are themselves held together by electromagnetic forces, the form of which contemporary physics has been unable to determine, or even whether they exist or not! Yet, and here is the paradox, it takes enormous presence of mind—both literal and metaphorical—to fully understand the condition of emptiness. We need to comprehend absolutely the substance of things (a huge task in itself and one that may take many lifetimes) before we can grasp their inherent emptiness. Once we realize that the nature of sin is fundamentally insubstantial and empty and is created by the mind, the mind is at rest and sin disappears.

To continue the elemental analogy, it is as if the Buddhist practitioner is a miner, searching for gold. She or he enters deep into the shaft and discovers the gold. The gold, however is impure, covered in dust and rock and clustered about with other elements. In order to get to the gold, it is important to remove the layers of other elements and then, once the gold is retrieved, it is necessary to refine the gold of its impurities. This is what Buddhists would mean by repentance—a washing away of impurities and refinement of the self. This is another aspect of the bodhisattva vow: that no matter how infinite the defilements are, he or she vows to extinguish them.

It is worth exploring in more detail the issue of the

punishment for those who do bad things. To contemporary Buddhists such as myself, the idea of realms of heaven seems a somewhat archaic way of trying to understand what happens to people who did bad things before they died. The way I see it making sense to people today is to say that the murderer is also the victim of his own bad energy—his unhappiness, his disturbed mind, and his hatred are in themselves forms of punishment.

Some people may conceive that, because it believes in karma and stillness, Buddhism teaches passivity and acceptance of evil rather than actively trying to stop it. This is wrong. Buddhism recognizes that while we—by which I mean the human race—are the same, we're also different. We live in different spheres with different influences, even though those influences are interconnected. There are some people who want to destroy other people and they need to be stopped.

From a Buddhist perspective, stopping people from making bad karma is necessary. A Mahayana Buddhist text entitled *Upaya-kausalya Sutra* depicts a bodhisattva sea captain named Maha Karuna who, in order to save the other five hundred passengers, has to kill a robber who is trying to murder all the people on the boat. This may seem a shocking event for those who believe that Buddhism only advocates nonviolence. Even in extreme situations such as the above story, where many more lives will be spared if one is killed, the karma that Maha Karuna will take on himself will be a heavy one. And that is exactly the point. The bodhisattva needs to take responsibility for the result of negative karma caused by his action of killing the robber. He was aware of that burden, and knew how his action needed the judgment of wisdom and consequence to be carried out. The question remains for those of us who are not bodhisattvas and don't consider our actions as deeply as the captain: What kind of action is considered appropriate?

Killing bad people may get rid of individuals, but it doesn't get rid of the causes of the individuals' actions or the results of what those individuals did. It is, in other words, only a short-term solution. As we have seen over and over again, killing one person can generate many future killers who see that one person as a martyr. Buddhism itself balances such individual action with the recognition that we're all connected, all dependent. We always need to ask ourselves, why. Buddhism is very practical and realistic about motivation and outcome. Two stories told by the Buddha highlight how realistic Buddhism is when it comes to establishing right and wrong behavior.

At the time of the Buddha, there was a prince called Jeta, who'd received the five precepts from the Buddha: not to kill, not to steal, not to be sexually promiscuous or wanton, not to lie, and not to drink intoxicants. The prince, however, was finding the fifth one hard to keep, because as a prince he led a very social life. So the prince went to the Buddha and told him he didn't want to uphold the five precepts. "I want to change," he said.

"When you drink are you really happy?" the Buddha asked.

"No, I'm always worrying about the five precepts."

"Don't worry," the Buddha said. "Because your mind is not indulgent when you drink, you're not violating the five precepts."

We call this, the "leaky good." While the prince is being good, like a roof that goodness is leaky. It's an imperfect good. What we can learn from this is not that you reluctantly or grudgingly act for the good but that, if you're breaking your own precepts, your mind should not be indulgent in the activity.

Another story the Buddha told concerns Queen Malika. Malika's husband, the Emperor, was very hungry but didn't like his chef's food. So much did he dislike the food that he threatened to have his chef taken out and beheaded. When Malika, who had received the five precepts, heard of this she prepared a meal and dressed herself in her most gorgeous clothes. Accompanying the Emperor, she invited him for a drink and to feast. The Emperor was surprised.

"You observe the five precepts," he said. "Why today are you deciding to drink?"

"I'm in a good mood and wish for your company in enjoying this wine and food," she replied.

The Emperor, after he'd dined with the Queen, turned to her and said, "This food is not good. Where's my chef?" Then he realized he'd given orders for him to be killed and regretted his haste. The Queen told the Emperor that she'd protected the cook and that he wasn't dead. Far from being angry at Malika's deception, the Emperor was delighted that his order hadn't been carried out. Once more, the Queen performed an imperfect good, breaking one precept in order to save someone's life.

What these stories show is that living in this world and alleviating the suffering of others is always challenging, for it may involve compromises with one's own sense of right and wrong. Nevertheless, Buddhism demands action. It demands action even when we're not perfectly able to conduct ourselves with absolute probity in all aspects of our life. Since Buddhism believes we're all connected, it doesn't hold that anyone is truly perfect, because karma binds us all together. The bodhisattva vow is one that seeks out suffering and seeks to remedy it. It doesn't expect us to dwell on our own self-righteousness or lock ourselves away from the realities of life.

This is why we need to be humble about our responses to evil acts. We need to reflect on their causes, without attachment and blame. We need, reasonably and responsibly, to take on the bad karma ourselves and see how we in some way might have been to blame for some aspects of the tragedy that's befallen us. In sum, we need to think about the laws of cause and effect, for that is where the mystery lies. As Venerable Master Hsing Yun, says: "God is in the laws of cause and effect."

Buddhism's recognition of dependence removes the

abstraction from the term "evil" and makes what we consider evil both easier to get our heads around and yet more challenging to combat. Because of the realization of interdependence, evil becomes something to which we're attached and in some way responsible for. Because we're in some way connected to that evil, it's therefore more easily conquerable than a demonic abstraction would be. Evil is thus rendered both more immediate and menacing, because it lurks within us all as a consequence of our actions, and, paradoxically, precisely because it is here and now, among and within us, it is more vulnerable to being challenged and turned into something good.

Let me give you an analogy. Consider the turning on of a light in a dark room. All the furniture, decorations, and elements of the room were present before the light switch was flicked on. But it takes illumination—and we need to have the wisdom of turning on the light—to see and appreciate them. Conversely, the darkness that we thought was so encompassing, that seemed so thick and impenetrable, the darkness that offered no hope of a way out from despair, is seen to be what it is: merely the absence of light; in itself, nothing. The darkness has not *gone* anywhere; simply the condition has changed. In a similar way, evil is simply a conditioned absence of light. If we simply flick the switch—alter the condition—then the evil will disappear. The challenge exists in finding the switch when we are enveloped in darkness, unable to see anything, ignorant of which way to turn, groping vainly for something we know, stumbling against shapes that hurt us and feel unfamiliar to us. Changing the condition may be simple; finding our way to that understanding is hard.

6 ❀ War and Peace?

In a talk I was giving once, a young man asked me, "Why do leaders today act unpeacefully?" It was a poignant question, a plea almost. But it is not just leaders who act unpeacefully. All of us at times act out of anger and fear and bring suffering upon someone else whom we think is causing *us* suffering.

With the freedom we have in the West—and, indeed, the freedom we have as human beings—comes responsibility. This is why we should never confuse freedom with independence, even though we think that freedom *only* comes about through independence. It is thinking this way that has led to the worst forms of nationalism and racism. Such independence encourages narrowness and isolationism, arrogance and ignorance. True freedom comes about when we recognize that we are all interdependent. We need to declare our *inter*dependence.

Freedom based on a false sense of independence is often a projection of our own identity on the world. Because we are anxious about our own identities and purpose, clinging on to what we believe we are, we try to control others. This is why the heart of conflict resolution is putting ourselves in someone else's position and trying to see things from their point of view. Changing our position, altering our perspective, adopting a different stance—all these things can force us to rethink our own rigid positions about our identity and purpose and sense of independence. Putting ourselves in someone else's shoes is a very good way of stopping violence, whether on a personal or a national level.

This is why, instead of a leadership based on partisanship and conducting policies and programs that work only to promote the interests of a select group of people or even the nation state, we need a leadership of compassion where policies and programs are created that promote the interests of as many individuals as possible, extending beyond the nation state to the whole world. We do not need a leadership of superpowers clashing but a leadership of compassion whose goal is world peace. Instead of a narrow nationalism we need a universal patriotism. We need to honor and defend the *patria*, or homeland, that is this planet, on which we all depend.

Of course, like everyone, I am shocked and sorrowful when terrorists strike. I feel angry and my heart seeks retribution when people are killed or wounded by a bomb going off. Yet, in these times of interconnectivity—where we can travel around the world and communicate with people instantaneously over the telephone or Internet, where countries are filled with peoples of different religious, cultural, or ethnic background and there are mixed-race children—we need to ask ourselves, what is the meaning of the nation state and an identity solely bound up with a piece of land or an idea of nationhood when you could be attacked anywhere or by anyone? In its terrible, negative way, terrorism is showing us that we are all connected. What if we were to respond in such a way that we turned that sense of connection where no one is safe into one where we're connected and all are safe?

Yet, when the young man asked me, "Why do leaders today act unpeacefully?" I found it hard to answer honestly, because I wasn't sure that he was ready to hear an opinion different from the answer he wanted. Indeed, many of us merely want to hear the things we already agree with, to feel assured and comforted that someone wise is taking care of us. But Buddhism is very clear about the responsibilities and needs of peace: violence creates violence and peace creates peace, and we are *all* responsible for creating both. If we only look narrowly at a situation then we'll fail to make a positive impact; the more widely and deeply we look, and the greater our forethought and genuine consideration of others, the more successful we'll be in creating peace and security.

It's my belief that the best protection for all of us, no matter on which piece of land we live, is an acknowledgment of the common condition that is our interdependence.

Operating from that belief will lead us to practices that make it possible for positive relationships to grow and negative consequences to diminish. Once we realize that our efforts to project who we are and what we believe onto the world are futile, we'll stop expecting or even desiring others to be like us. When we stop expecting and desiring others to be like us there is less resistance, less confusion, and less confrontation, which then may make people want to be like us of their own accord. It's important to remember that Buddhism has the distinction of being the only major world religion that has never engaged in holy wars. Could it be otherwise for a belief system that has written in its scriptures, "Buddhism is in the midst of respectfulness"?

The life of the ancient Buddhist king Asoka is a great example of the relationship between leadership, respect, and a prosperous community. The conversion of King Asoka to Buddhism ushered in an age of splendor in India. As a result of his conversion, he refrained from his previous habits of killing and conquering; he reduced taxes and respected all religions, and even ushered in animal welfare practices. His subjects loved him, and the nation grew wealthy and strong. As Venerable Master Hsing Yun points out about Asoka's kingdom, "Tolerating differences will not lead to division. It will only increase vitality and bring in fullness and blossoming." The five fingers of the hand are different, some long and some shorter. Each finger working alone can only perform a limited number of tasks; working together, they can perform miracles. This is the message that all of us, including our leaders, need to understand. If we adopt such practices, then all of us have the potential to become Asokas.

Recognizing our interdependence forces us to go and engage with the world and not retreat from it. It also allows us liberation from attachment to permanence by freeing us from the impossibility of change and potentially freeing us from the disappointments that belief in permanence constantly creates for us. I've already indicated that our conditionality, our full interdependence with each other and the world around us, can allow us to relate our suffering to that of other living beings by making their suffering our own. But it can also make us aware that our own suffering is merely a condition that can be alleviated by recognizing that that feeling, too, can change.

Buddhism is not about withdrawing from the world. To the contrary, we can all change the world. But we need to know that we change *with* the world, and that that "we" is constantly changing *in* the world. From this, comes true leadership.

7 ❦ Compassion and Wisdom

Buddhism argues that compassion is generated by seeing that everything is interrelated. If my finger is hurt, it affects how I behave. If I knock my hand, I will feel uncomfortable. I might not be able to work; I might have a headache. The suffering I experience is not localized merely to my finger.

Such a mindset is infinitely applicable. For instance, I can recognize that a Chinese woman may feel anger and resentment about what happened to her during the Cultural Revolution. She is a victim. She is a victim in the same way that the Tibetans are victims. Even murderers and perpetrators of injustice are victims, in that they suffer because their minds are polluted. The conditions that surround them lead them to make wrong judgments. I realize that this is very controversial: but even suicide bombers are victims of their blind faith and biased judgment. They and their families need our compassion, too.

That last statement should give us an insight into how tough-minded true compassion is, how strong-willed and disciplined need to be our minds and hearts to practice it truly. True compassion is not pity or weakness. It is not about feeling better about yourself or forgetting what someone has done. It doesn't even necessarily mean being forgiving. It means extending ourselves into the mind of the person who has done us or others harm and recognizing that that person is conditioned by his or her background. Consider this: Look at the children around us, even the ones in our own homes. Without doubt, some of them will grow up to do terrible things. But do we believe for one moment that they are born to become murderers or rapists? Of course not. That is why when we try and profile killers we should recognize that they were conditioned and that everybody in one way or another contributed to that conditioning.

I cannot emphasize enough that this understanding of conditioning shouldn't be an excuse to avoid responsibility. Buddhism doesn't deny individual responsibility. The Buddhist insights that we're all conditioned, that the self is dependent, and that all is impermanent, don't mean that the perpetrator can claim that, since everything is conditioned and coexistent, he doesn't bear any responsibility for his actions. As I suggested in my chapter on karma, all actions—whether good or bad—produce karma; and karma is not only collective, it's also individual. While we're not totally free in our actions, we're not totally dependent either. Like Christianity, Buddhism understands that human beings have free will. Because we're interdependent, however, Buddhism places free will within the context of the interdependence of other beings. Because we're interdependent, we're in some way *all* responsible for *all* actions all the time.

In seeking to understand the nature of the mind and suffering, Buddhists attempt to discover the purer part of themselves and so make the will to be good that much stronger. Through disciplines such as meditation, the Buddhist seeks to make judgments about existence that are less skewed by bias or clouded with impure thoughts or conceptions. The challenge of the Buddhist practitioner is to peel away the layers of illusion that cloud his or her judgment. This great task is accomplished by the exercise of free will; in turn, it enlarges the power and purity of that will. Unlike Christianity, Buddhism doesn't see free will as a gift from God. Like everything else, free will is conditioned. This places even more emphasis on us to exercise our free will responsibly—to cause less harm and promote more good. I'll discuss meditation and the mind in more detail in later chapters.

Buddhism binds all our deeds together so that every deed—no matter how trivial—is consequential. Thus action, of any sort, needs to be the well-considered offshoot of a pure mind, if the consequences are to be good for you, let alone anyone or anything else. This is how compassion is bound up with wisdom.

Compassion is not merely about being good to others, it's about making our own lives easier and happier. Compassion generates wisdom because it allows us to move beyond the merely sensuous understanding of the world to insight and perception. Wisdom requires attentiveness. It's like being handed a glass full of murky water, shaken constantly by our karmic activities. First, we need to let the glass stop shaking and the water to become motionless. Then, slowly, the dust particles will begin to sink to the bottom of the glass and the water will begin to clear. The sediment doesn't disappear. It's merely more clearly seen. Likewise, suffering and evil—all those conditions that cloud our clear perception—don't disappear. They become more visible, and thus more easily contained.

Our challenge as Buddhists is to let the water become stilled. In Buddhism, we have a saying: If a pond is murky, it is hard to see the moon. I'd add that, even worse than that, if a pond is murky, and we are creating waves, then the moon is not only hard to see, but the moon's shape—when it is glimpsed—is distorted. The only thing worse than not being able to see clearly, is to think we're seeing something clearly when we are not.

I remember visiting a cave in Virginia with some friends. At the very bottom of the tunnel there was an underground lake with water so clear that it was almost impos-

sible to see the water. Only if we touched this unpolluted
water did we see the shimmering of the clear liquid. Likewise, in Buddhism, if the mind is clear then it is possible to
reflect things as they are, without distortion or without a
distance between us and the thing reflected upon. But this
can only come about when there is stillness and we stop
shaking things up.

This is why Buddhism teaches us not to rush to judgment about people. We're always making judgments about
people and things, and they're often wrong. Not only are they
inaccurate—outpourings of our own anxieties, fears, prejudices, and ignorance—but they're usually founded on pieces
rather than the whole. One day I may like my partner; the
next day he or she might drive me crazy. Everywhere we
look we're given signals by society about who's good and
who's bad, what's heroic and what's not. It is a very simplistic,
one-sided view of things that only perpetuates a distorted
view of reality. Life isn't like that: the good and the bad don't
always do good or bad things.

In Buddhism, to repeat, there's no such thing as a good
and bad person; there are only good or bad deeds. Thinking
this way means that we cannot set the "evil-doer" outside of
our own life and say that he or she has nothing to do with
us. We cannot say that we bear no responsibility for their actions. We cannot determine that that person is possessed by
something we could never be possessed by. Instead, we have
to examine our own lives, our own bad deeds, our own re-

sponsibility for generating bad karma. We have to grapple with the possibility that we, too, think thoughts that could generate harm. We cannot escape our responsibility.

This is why the search for wisdom within Buddhism is so hard. It is relentlessly honest. Truly Buddhist thought doesn't settle on a point and say that every problem has been solved. Every moment is filled with the possibility of good and bad actions because we're conditioned, interdependent, and impermanent. Wisdom is recognizing those conditions and becoming clear-minded about them. And it is about the cultivation of that clear thinking and understanding personal suffering that I talk about in the remainder of the book.

8 ❃ The Eight Kinds of Suffering

Siddhartha Gautama's spiritual journey to understand the nature of suffering involved two key components that directly impact on our own. First, he moved from the utmost luxury to the utmost deprivation, and then realized that neither of them provided the solution. This is why Buddhism is called the Middle Way—and why it is skeptical of the claims of truth, revelation, or knowledge that come from extremes. The second is that the Buddha's aim was not merely personal salvation, nor even the salvation of all other people, but the salvation of all sentient beings.

While Buddhism is, as I have said, very practical, at its center it also places emphasis on right understanding and right thinking. According to Buddhist thought, before there can be right action, there has to be right thought, and right thought depends on a correct analysis of the conditions of your own life and existence in general. This is why, in order to understand suffering, it's necessary to comprehend the nature of the mind and the nature of the self. Buddhism's insights into consciousness and the mind and the self are one of its great gifts to humankind. First, we will look at the categories of suffering.

Buddhism has categorized suffering in different ways to emphasize their different aspects. In some Buddhist traditions, suffering is divided in two ways. One type of suffering is that which comes from outside of us—for example, assault, accidents, disease, natural disasters, and other calamities. The other is the suffering that is generated from inside of us. This suffering might be a sense of dissatisfaction when, for instance, we want more than we have been given or we're not happy with who we are. This is a basic division. Among many other types of divisions Buddhism splits suffering into eight different categories. This chapter will spend some time with each type of suffering, since they bear directly on our daily lives and I believe offer some insight into how we can reframe the problems suffering creates.

The First Kind of Suffering

The first kind of suffering is caused by birth. People often see birth as a joyful event—the bringing of new life into the world, the experience of parenthood, the feeling that one's family will continue beyond one's own death. All of these experiences are, indeed, potentially full of joy, and are to be honored. Nevertheless, birth is also attended by much suffering. In many countries around the world the act of giving birth is surrounded by great pain and also a substantial amount of mortality. Many babies and mothers die in childbirth because they don't have access to basic hygiene or sterile implements; there may be complications in the position of the fetus or because of the mother's loss of blood. The Buddha's own mother died in childbirth, and his aunt raised him. Even if the birth is free of complications and there are midwives and doctors in attendance, the experience of giving birth is excruciatingly painful—so much so that Western medicine has created drugs such as epidural injections to numb the body. No matter how free we are from pain, however, the absence of pain in childbirth should tell us something about the life we're entering into and how much pain we'll experience and wish to avoid.

In addition to childbirth itself there is the fact that the baby him- or herself is moving from the womb, where it has existed in a comfortable, sealed environment, into a new world, which is different and strange. This is why the baby is crying. I should make clear here that when Buddhism in the First Noble Truth talks about all life being suffering, it doesn't necessarily mean that, even though we enter this world in shock and in some suffering, we *have* to end our life in suffering. Indeed, Buddhism is about diminishing or neutralizing the suffering that's inherent in life's passages. Yet, even though it may be good for a baby to exercise its lungs as soon as it's born, that she or he does so by crying rather than laughing somehow points to a primal recognition of suffering that Buddhism makes its First Noble Truth.

In April 2000, I was invited by UNICEF to participate in their Safe Motherhood Project. I was there as a consultant to help attendees understand why, from the cultural standpoint, the rate of maternal mortality in South Asia was so high in comparison with the maternal mortality rate of Europe. I have learned that some of the cultural reasons for such a situation might be that people thought the blood was impure and that women were deemed not valuable. This meant that when women gave birth they reacted extremely negatively to all of the blood, or the husbands of the women in childbirth would rather their wife die so they could take another wife, with another dowry. It may seem incredible to hear that these things still exist in the world in the twenty-first century, but it occurs in some countries in South Asia. Even people working in the hospitals can be alarmingly indifferent to the rights of women and children, which leads to the death of too many of them. When the very first stages of life are greeted with such indifference or even hostility, how can we deny the presence of suffering in birth?

It has always been the case, and it remains so today, that the lives of children are deeply threatened and vulnerable. Children have always relied on adults to provide them with food and care, yet more and more it seems children are under threat. They are physically, sexually, or emotionally abused;

they are abandoned in dumpsters or left to fend for themselves on the streets. They are sold into slavery (in parts of Africa and Asia), forced to enter the sex trade (for instance, in Thailand and Cambodia), compelled to become thieves or drug carriers or, even worse, coerced into being soldiers (such as in Sierra Leone). Some are kidnapped and trained to be suicide bombers, as is the case with the Tamil Tigers in Sri Lanka. Others are abandoned to the streets and left to fend for themselves, where they live by scavenging and theft, high on glue that they sniff and prey for the unscrupulous or sometimes even the police. Others suffer from malnutrition or from obesity; they are deprived of the simplest staples in their lives or bombarded with images and messages that make them feel inadequate. From the richest mansions of the United States to the poorest back streets of India, children are increasingly on their own. And, as recent reports have made clear, children—along with their mothers—constitute by far the majority of the world's poor.

How does Buddhism look at the phenomenon of the suffering of birth and childhood? In Chinese Buddhism, there is no such thing as a birthday. Instead of calling it a "birthday" we call it "the day our mother suffered"—a way of reminding us that suffering attends our existence from our first moments, and that it's a suffering somehow shared between mother and child. A birthday is, thus, considered a day to reflect with gratitude on the sacrifices our mother has made for us.

In this way, Buddhism examines our tendency toward, on the one hand, sentimentality and, on the other, closed-heartedness when it comes to the lives of children other than our own. It advocates compassion based on the experience of *all* children—whether they're ours or not. It demands that we be responsible for them and recognize that their lives are precious and their fears genuine, no matter the circumstances they're born in. When we think this way, we should see it as our responsibility that forty million children around the world have AIDS, or that many millions of children face starvation and illness every day all around the world. They're our children, too.

The Second Kind of Suffering

The second suffering has to do with aging, one of the conditions that Siddhartha Gautama came upon when riding in his coach. It should be obvious why aging is associated with suffering. We find it harder to walk and do the things we used to do. We get tired more easily, and men worry about losing their hair and women about having more wrinkles. Our minds may forget things and, as happens to the unfortunate ones among us, we may suffer from some form of dementia. For those of us whose minds remain strong and alert, it is an exquisite feature of the suffering of aging that we conceive of ourselves as young and vital while our body tells us we're otherwise.

Of course, there are great gifts in growing older: we

have wisdom and experience; we have garnered some respect from society and achieved a position in the world. But society, especially in the West, isn't particularly concerned to venerate the elderly or value their contribution. It's obsessed with the young or the new; with the precocious and the flamboyant. The knowledge and depth of history available to the young from those who've seen some of the recurring follies of the past are, unfortunately, rarely drawn upon by the younger generations. Even for those of us who are treated with deference or honor, aging, unfortunately, doesn't pause to pay its respects. Nor does it hold itself back because we've achieved something within society! Clearly, there is suffering in aging.

The Third Kind of Suffering

The third category of suffering in Buddhism is sickness and disease. Sickness and disease are not only physical but they can also be mental. All involve suffering, even though that suffering may be different in scope or degree. The categories of physical and mental suffering also not only encompass the ailments of cancer, diabetes, or other types of physical disabilities, or dementia or Alzheimer's and other sorts of mental diseases, but they include the psychological pain involved when we're debilitated by disease—such as when paraplegics or quadriplegics are unable to move their bodies as their mind wishes or people who've suffered strokes are paralyzed on one side of their body. As with the previous kind of suffering, such suffering is about the inability to do the things we once could, even though our mind is sharp and wants us to be able to move.

Likewise, such suffering can also involve the suffering of the loss of dignity, such as when the body does things we don't want it to do—when we're incontinent or have nervous tics or when the synapses and nerve endings send incorrect signals from and to the brain. In such a situation, the physical suffering we're undergoing is compounded by our embarrassment and our fear of dependency.

The Fourth Kind of Suffering

The fourth category is death. Death is not only the suffering we are ourselves undergoing as we die but the suffering of the people around us who love us and don't want us to leave them. Buddhism describes death as a time when our consciousness leaves the body and compares it to a turtle leaving its shell or a snake peeling the skin. Buddhists believe that it is painful for the consciousness to leave the body—irrespective of whether our death is attended by injury, disease, or physical pain—because our physical body is that to which we are most obviously attached. As such, our karmic bond to it is that much greater.

People come to me looking for reassurance when someone they love is dying and they've had to watch them fading away or when they're dying themselves and are scared. At moments such as these, it is hard to grasp the truth that we're impermanent and that all of us, whether rich or poor, saint or sinner, will have to die. Even when we're confronted by the reality of death, we like to believe that we're immortal. It was hard to offer these dying people or their caregivers counsel. As we see every day, people die easily.

When those confronting death come to me, however, I advise them that, while it's right to be sad at the fact of death, it's also important to try and conceive of death in a different manner. Zhuangzi, a Daoist philosopher who lived in China many centuries ago, himself experienced loss when his wife died. Zhuangzi reacted by banging a drum and singing joyfully. People around him thought he'd gone mad. But he told them that life was a circle of birth and death, and that death was the beginning of a birth. If you didn't die, he told them, how could you be reborn? This was why he was celebrating: his wife was going to have a new life.

Zhuangzi was a remarkable man. Not many of us could be as easy-going. Yet, we have to prepare ourselves for the fact that we will die and have to detach ourselves from our sense of our own immortality. We need to be prepared for the fact that life is always changing. Again, this is hard. Not only are we emotionally attached, but we're psychologically attached: we cannot believe that the one we love is dying—whether it is someone else or ourselves.

One of the gifts of Buddhism and Chinese culture has been the acceptance of death and the preparation for it. We Buddhists prepare for our death every day in order to make it as peaceful as possible. Our temples are serene havens for people who are frustrated and angered by their jobs and lives.

One of the things I always suggest to people is that they should try and create a mental temple everywhere they are. Once in our metaphorical temple we can release the unwholesome thoughts of anger, hatred, frustration, and sadness. We can then cherish these moments of peace throughout the day. Cultivating thoughts of peace will prepare us better for the inevitable day when we will pass from this life.

The Fifth Kind of Suffering

The fifth category is the suffering of departing from the people we love. This suffering occurs not only when we die. For instance, we might have recently got married and then had to go to work or somewhere else, leaving our loved one behind. This kind of suffering is particularly subtle, because not only is there the suffering of leaving someone behind, but there's the suffering of knowing that when we're with them, after pining for them, we'll still have to leave them. So we suffer when we're away from them, and we suffer when we're with them by knowing that we have to depart from each other some time. This kind of suffering challenges in a very intense way our attachment to loved ones by forcing us to acknowledge our dependence on them and, indeed, our interdependence with them.

The Sixth Kind of Suffering

The sixth kind of suffering is one that many people who are new to Buddhism find very entertaining. It's the suffering of being with somebody we hate. We may work in a company and have a colleague whom we dislike intensely, but we need to be with him or her because our job demands it or our boss requires us to work with that person. Or we may live next to someone who makes a lot of noise and keeps us awake at night with their partying. In fact, isn't it the case that we find ourselves spending the same amount of time with the colleague we dislike as we do with the loved one we miss so much? Sometimes we may feel it's even more! This suffering only enhances our feelings of suffering at not being with the one we want to be with while increasing our resentment at being with the one we hate.

What both the fifth and sixth kinds of suffering point to is that our human relationships are fraught with false expectations and needless confrontations. It's not too much to say that all the problems we suffer from in relationships come down to attachment. Many of us enter relationships—whether intimate or otherwise—believing that we need to have a partner so we can have self-esteem. My students often feel they need to have a boyfriend or a girlfriend in order to feel good about themselves. Or businesspeople may feel that they have to be respected and revered by their workers or their clients in order to feel they're successful or powerful.

What these experiences come down to is that many of us feel that unless we're loved and recognized by another person we're not worth anything. As far as dealing with day-to-day suffering, I think it's very important that we love and recognize our own worth from inside us, so that no matter whether anybody loves us or not, no matter whether our loved one leaves us for someone else or is torn away from us in a disaster or through an illness, we know for ourselves that we are good, and their departure is not necessarily our fault or a consequence of our behavior.

Under these categories of suffering is loneliness. The sense of being isolated, unloved, misunderstood, and with no connection to anyone or anything can be a profound form of suffering, because it is based on our self-identity as much as it might be because we have been widowed or abandoned or scorned by society and our family and friends. We need to have compassion for the lonely, and the lonely need to have compassion for themselves. All of us need to reach out to each other, extend a hand, or provide a shoulder to lean or cry on. In reaching out, we ourselves are enriched; the more we give to others, the more likely they are to give to us when we need them.

Some might say that by saying we need to value ourselves I'm abandoning our recognition of conditionality in favor of individualism. Not so. If we recognize our self-worth we become more lovable because we are in turn more generous to others. Confidence in the self is a confidence that has a potential to give more because it comes from a sounder foundation. Clearly, arrogance and pride are states of mind whereby the self has forgotten its conditionality in favor of self-aggrandizement. Karma will probably dictate that the arrogant and proud individual will be brought down through his or her own actions, if not in this lifetime then in later ones. Nevertheless, Buddhism agrees with the human potential movement in calling for a centered self that can give so much to the world because it doesn't need to take so much to survive.

Both the fifth and sixth forms of suffering concern our relationships. This is one of the other major causes of suffering. I am always struck by the fact that many people look for quantity rather than quality in their intimate relationships, focusing on pleasure and desire rather than happiness. My students in Taiwan surprise me when they tell me they're actively looking to have one-night stands. While having sex may be physically harmless if all the precautions about sexually transmitted diseases are taken, we simply don't know how others will be affected psychologically by such behavior. As French philosopher and theologian Blaise Pascal (1623–1662) once said, "The heart has its reasons of which reason knows nothing," and the consequences of our having a one-night stand with someone might lead that person to become emotionally attached and fall in love with us. She or he might become hurt by our subsequent indifference. We ourselves might fall in love and be hurt in turn.

Once more, we have to acknowledge the laws of cause and effect. Our sexuality is a powerful signal of who we are and triggers lots of emotions. Being so casual about it is sure to incur consequences, and we should be prepared to respond to them. We need to ask ourselves what we truly want from our intimate relationships. It seems to me that we should want to have no intimate relationships at all rather than ones that are bad or self-destructive.

The consequences of our sexual behavior and our sense of the need to be loved can be positive. But they can also be very negative. For instance, I've been stunned at the amount of domestic violence there is in the world, even in the West. It's violence that cuts across class and race. Clearly, there's great trauma and suffering associated with the need to acquire and control in our relationships. It's as if we're trying to find out about ourselves or express ourselves, but we're doing it in the wrong way. We're attaching our self-worth to money or power or status and trying to prove we're a better person because we have a better job, or a prettier wife, or a faster car. We somehow believe that acquisition means happiness, even though the real person—the one behind the big suit, or the high-walled mansion, or the dark windows in the stretch limo—has the same emotional and physical needs as the poorest, least influential person in society. Essentially, we've forgotten not only our needs but who we are. When, in some way, we realize that none of these things makes us happy, we seem to lash out at whoever is near us.

We need to go back to ourselves and ask ourselves those questions: Who are we? What do we really want? Why are we on this planet? If we can access our inner wealth, the enormous treasures that we have inside us, then we'll never be poor or unimportant. Buddhism has a saying that reflects this knowledge. We are like a poor child who has millions of pearls in his or her pocket but doesn't know what they are or how to use them. Our wealth is right there within us. We simply need to be able to recognize it and use it properly.

The richness of inner wealth balances the poverty of external wealth. The more we have inside the less we'll need to have on the outside to buttress our sense of inner worth. Possessions then become things we can give away or use to the benefit of all beings rather than ways to make us feel good about ourselves. The truly wealthy person doesn't need to prove how important or intelligent or wealthy he or she is. Likewise, the truly poor person will always be showing us how much they have. They may not be equal in material terms, but Buddhism believes that everyone is equal in inner treasure.

The Seventh Kind of Suffering

The seventh category of suffering is one that was touched upon when I mentioned the two types of suffering; it is the suffering that comes from not having the things we want. We may want to be the president of the company but we don't get chosen, or we want to be a politician but we don't get voted in, or we may want to have a car but we cannot afford one, or we're addicted to drugs and we can't get an extra supply. Likewise, we may love someone but they don't love us. This is one of the most common forms of suffering, and it's caused by craving and attachment.

Many people in the West have two major misconceptions about Buddhism. The first one is that Buddhism believes it's wrong to have possessions. The second is that Buddhism believes that everything you have should be unadorned. As to the second misconception: Buddhism doesn't want everything to be simple and plain. Buddhism responds to beauty. Nor do things need to be bland; they can be luxurious, vibrant with colors, and produced with great skill and artifice. I always encourage people to respect beauty and craftsmanship. I see craftsmanship and even mechanical sophistication as artistic expressions. For instance, a really beautiful car or a highly crafted watch is to be admired for its expressiveness as well as its mechanical complexity. Buddhism is not about blandness.

What Buddhism asks us to do—and this relates to the first misconception—is to keep remembering interdependence. Thus, for instance, if we drive a very expensive car but it has a very inefficient or polluting engine, then we need to acknowledge our responsibility in polluting the planet and consuming natural resources that might be used by other beings. The car itself—the chassis, the stylings, the artistry of the interior—might not be the problem, the engine and its consumption is, as could be our use of it. Do we need to drive to the corner store, or could we walk instead?

This is why I feel strongly that cathedrals and temples have a role in fostering feelings of the divine. Some people feel that building temples or churches is a waste of money.

But I think the difference between a small hut and visiting the Vatican or a great temple is that the magnitude expresses and contains the divine. There is more awe, more reverence, as well as beauty. I wouldn't want all society to stagnate in sameness or blandness simply for the sake of homogeneity or plainness. But there needs to be restraint. For instance, we all love ivory and the craftsmanship that has gone into creating objects from that substance. But I don't think it is suitable to cause pain to animals by killing elephants to get it.

Buddhism asks us to make differentiations between the utility of an object and its beauty. Beauty doesn't consume. Therefore, possessions in and of themselves are not bad for Buddhists, even monks or nuns. While it's important to lead a simple life and follow the Middle Way, it's what we *do* with what we have rather than *what* we have that matters. Buddhism responds and respects variety—we're not all the same and not everyone needs to live exactly the same lifestyle. But when we affect the lives of other beings and the planet, then we need to have restraint and discipline.

This is how Buddhism responds to the phenomenon of consumption, and how Buddhism makes its accommodation with capitalism. Buddhism believes in the freedom of the individual to achieve his or her own goals, to follow his or her own mission in this world. The Buddha's choice of the Middle Way was at least partly brought about by his recognition that asceticism merely for its own sake was not bringing him any nearer to enlightenment any more than luxury was. But

Buddhism is mindful—and I use the word deliberately—of the suffering that is latent when we consume natural resources or the products of natural resources. In the case of ivory above, I've decided that, on consideration and based on the facts as I understand them, my pleasure at the craftsmanship and beauty of the product made with ivory wasn't worth the suffering of the living being that had to experience pain to have the ivory removed. This isn't a matter of utilitarian balancing between relative suffering. Buddhism sees our judgments as threads connected through time to all existence. In deciding what to do in a given situation, our behavior isn't merely juggling consequences as they occur to us, but living our lives fully in the recognition that everything we do has causes and consequences.

As a Buddhist, therefore, I try to reflect simplicity and beauty in everything I do. I respond to difference and artistry even as I practice my disciplines and pare down the inessentials. This is not a paradox, but more an interplay that is intrinsically Buddhist, because, to paraphrase Shakespeare's *Hamlet*, there is nothing either good or bad but action makes it so, and everything can be made beautiful or ugly by what we decide to do with it.

Becoming aware of the attachment we have to possessions and money is hard. Miserliness, as famously represented by Ebenezer Scrooge in Charles Dickens' *A Christmas Carol*, is a form of suffering. A similar fable from China relates the story of a man who lived very poorly but had a pile of gold ingots, which he wrapped in newspaper and hid under his bed. People who lived near the man knew he was rich but never saw him use any of his gold. One day, thieves broke into the man's house and stole all his gold. He was heartbroken. The man's neighbors, however, had no pity for him. "Since you never use the gold," they said, "why don't you take some bricks and wrap them in newspaper and then put them under your bed? What would be the difference?"

I like this story because I think too many of us don't use our money wisely or generously, we just like to see the numbers getting bigger in the bank. If death happens to us all, why simply accumulate money? This is not to say that the Buddhist promotes poverty. The point of this story is that we should be aware of attachment and wastefulness and assign value where it should be placed. There's another Buddhist saying that points out that even though we may have a thousand acres, every night we only need about six feet for sleep; and even though we have a hundred dishes for our food, we can only eat as much as will fill us up. So we need to enjoy the things we have and know our limits at the same time. We also need to acknowledge our appetites—acquisitiveness, greed—and recognize our attachment to them. Only by doing that will we be able to detach ourselves from them and save ourselves and others much suffering.

The Eighth Kind of Suffering
The eighth kind of suffering is, in many ways, a summation

of all the suffering caused by our five aggregates, which are all the elements of our physical and mental make-up as well as sensation, conception, volition, and consciousness. We suffer physically and psychologically. We may be hungry and not have enough food, we're thirsty and don't have enough water, or we need shelter but are homeless. Even when we are hungry and are body is satisfied, we will still suffer because the sensory pleasures themselves are so short and we will become hungry again. Feeling full itself is, therefore, a testament to impermanence. Even the buying of a new car or a house will give us pleasure for only a short period of time. As Daoist philosopher Laozi says, "Our great suffering is because we have this body." Because of this body we experience aging, sickness, and death, and in our mind we also endure suffering because we're forced to see the changes our body is going through.

Now, some might say that, having discussed all the different modes of suffering listed above, that the world and their lives are not always characterized by suffering. And in this they may be correct—because we *do* know joy, and there are moments when that experience is not just ours, or our families, or even our nation's. However, even joyful or happy sensations can bring about suffering, because they too will not last forever. Once more, we have to take into account the impermanence of all things. Furthermore, suffering is also created by the change from happiness to unhappiness and back again. At times, we may feel neither happy nor sad, but neutral. Everything is in flux between states. The recognition of impermanence and flux is its own kind of suffering.

All these modes of suffering are caused by desire, hatred, or ignorance. Desire reflects on when we want to have more or be with someone else. Hatred obviously refers to those we hate but who are present with us; and illusion or ignorance is about how we don't expect impermanence in our mind but it constantly comes back to us. And these three are connected: Desire creates attachment; dislike creates hatred; craving creates disgust; and ignorance creates all of them. All depend on a failure to perceive the true nature of the self, which is what I will discuss next.

9 ❋ Who Suffers?

We talk about ourselves a lot; we also talk about our *selves* a lot. But, what exactly is the self? And how is it possible to talk about it? Certainly, we can talk about our achievements and actions. But am I simply just the combination of everything I've done in my life? Is that really *who* I am?

In my second year of high school, I was too busy with extracurricular activities to be a good student and fell from being top in my class to fifty-sixth. For someone with as strong an ethic of work and study as myself, it was a huge shock. I didn't know whether I was really the first person who'd sunk to fifty-sixth or the fifty-sixth person who'd miraculously been first for a while. Even though it was hard to detach myself from *feeling* belittled or aggrieved at my lowly status, that was the first inkling I had that where I was ranked had nothing to do with *me*; it was all about the effort and time I put in. I wish I could say I became much less competitive. However, I became just as anxious and competitive when I undertook my Ph.D.!

We find it very hard not to define ourselves by our achievements. You might be a movie star who, by the time you are seventeen years old, has earned enough money to buy a house in Beverly Hills. When you turn nineteen, however, you find you've lost all your money-earning potential and are washed up. You don't know whether you're the rich boy who lost lots of money or the poor boy who suddenly and temporarily became rich. This situation happens to many of us all the time. If we're laid off from work, are we someone who once belonged to a company and got fired, or were we someone who happened to work for that company for a short period of time? Are we still the manager we used to be, or someone who thought he or she was a manager but wasn't? Are we the unfortunate boss or lucky worker? Where is the real *I*—the true, unchanging, absolute *I*?

When I'm asked questions by my students about the meaning of the good life, I tell them that there is nothing wrong with money or fame or even power, but that we need to ask ourselves constantly: Am I happy with myself? Am I in control of myself? We should ask ourselves these questions before we set out on the road to wealth, prestige, and power. Then, should we achieve any or all of these things, we should ask the questions again. And when or if we lose any or all of these things or even become the reverse—poor, notorious, or powerless—we should ask ourselves the questions yet again. If, in all these three stages, we can know ourselves and manage ourselves, then we can do anything we set our heart on.

These examples show an obvious truth—one that the Buddha discovered after he returned to the palace and decided to become a renunciate: it is foolish to try and establish our identities, or seek happiness, solely through our social status. It won't protect us from suffering and it'll never fully satisfy us. Many of us try and run away from who we are, and cling to status as our identity. This is wrong: We're not the sum of how successful or unsuccessful we are in this life. We're not what other people think we are, or should be; and we shouldn't judge ourselves by how other people think we are.

Another truth that comes from the Buddha's realizations is that the physical body changes. The young prince Siddhartha gauged his own youthful beauty against the sick man and the old man and realized that his body would change just as those two individuals' bodies had changed. Yet we often feel our body is the most permanent thing we know. For instance, we look at ourselves in the mirror and there we are. We recognize ourselves. We're permanent. Indeed, we all know who we are. We're Peter or Mary and we are here, and, as if to confirm the solidity of our presence, people respond to us as though we were here as well.

But this permanence is an illusion. After all, we weren't once what we are now: we had a very different shape and identity when we were babies, or adolescents. We've all had those experiences of coming across a friend whom we haven't seen for many years and been unable to recognize him until he told us who he was. The question remains: Even though he looks completely different, is he still the same Michael whom we knew all those years previously?

There's a ghost story that illustrates what I mean. There was once a man, whom we'll call Mr. Johnson, who one night entered an abandoned house and discovered a dead body. Later on, he saw two ghosts entering the house. The first ghost saw the corpse and wanted to eat it; but the second ghost told the first that the corpse belonged to him, because he'd seen it first. The second ghost was larger, however, and tried to bully the first. While they were arguing, they glimpsed Mr. Johnson hiding in the corner. Unable to resolve their argument, the ghosts asked the terrified man to come over and judge who should eat the body. Because he'd seen the first ghost entering the house first, Mr. Johnson said that the dead body belonged to the first ghost. At this, the second ghost was so angry that he ripped off Mr. Johnson's arm and ate it. Immediately, the first ghost ripped an arm from the corpse and attached it to Mr. Johnson's body.

The second ghost then took another arm from Mr. Johnson and the first ghost attached the other arm from the corpse to Mr. Johnson's body. Part by part, the ghosts replaced Mr. Johnson's body with the dead one, leaving Mr. Johnson to wonder who he was. Was he still Mr. Johnson with the body of the dead man, or was he the dead man with the consciousness of Mr. Johnson?

While this story seems absurd, contemporary scientific endeavors are making this story a distinct possibility. Organ transplants and plastic surgery are becoming routine. What if our arms, kidneys, and hearts are artificial or transplanted from someone else? What happens if a majority, perhaps eighty percent, of our body has been changed? Are we still then who we were? Could we then claim that the physical body we see in the mirror is who we are? If our body changes as we age, and if our body changes because other bodies or body parts now make up our body, can we determine who or what that absolute self is that we think is *who* we are?

The quest for what precisely it is that makes us distinctly ourselves, the part of us that never changes, has perplexed and challenged philosophers of both the East and West for centuries. Some people say that it isn't the body where the self resides but in the feelings we have. We know who we are because we *feel* it. But as we've all experienced many times, feelings are very unreliable signposts of who we are. We feel hot and we get cold. We may rise in the morning feeling sad; a good breakfast may make us happy; and then we climb into our car and drive to work and hit a traffic jam and become angry. We're back to feeling sad again. To those who argue that it's the very fact we *feel* at all that makes us who we are, rather than particular feelings at any one time, I would argue that we should examine the nature of that feeling about feelings! How do we know that that feeling is not itself subject to change? The trouble with feelings is that they're so emotional! They *always* change. It seems to me to be obvious that, because we can feel so many emotions, locating the self within the emotions is not going to be satisfactory.

The French philosopher and mathematician René Descartes (1596–1650) famously said: "I think, therefore I am." Because of this, some people place the self in our capacity to think and in the thoughts themselves. However, our thoughts are even more changeable than our feelings. Part of the point of meditation, Buddhism recognizes, is to still the mind and somehow stop the plethora of thoughts that constantly arise and pass through our minds. After all, we're constantly changing our minds, thinking new things, acting impulsively without thinking things through, being literally "thought-less" (such as when we drive from one place to another without remembering any of the journey). How many relationships have been broken off or restarted because someone changed his or her mind? If the mind really is where our self resides, then all we can say is that the self is changeable.

Some people consider the memory to be the proper location of self. After all, our memories are carried across time—as the body changes, as our thoughts change, as our feelings change, our memories, so it is argued, are always with us, and thus remain where our identity is. But, then, how are we to account for people who lose their memory—whether permanently or temporarily? If we suffer from a temporary memory loss, does that mean we cease to be who we are? When a loved one gets Alzheimer's disease, some caregivers feel their loved ones are no longer the person they were, while others feel they are. Is it really the case that when we lose our memory our identity is lost as well?

A case study in how troubling the location of identity is, and how poignant is the loss of memory, can be found in Clive Wearing, a British conductor and broadcaster, who specialized in the complex music of the Renaissance. In 1985, Mr. Wearing became infected by encephalitis, which destroyed much of the hippocampus and frontal lobe areas of the brain. These are the places that scientists believe house our short-term memory. Thus, while Mr. Wearing was able to carry on normal long-term memory functions—such as walking, talking, writing, even playing and conducting music—whenever anybody stopped him and asked him what he was doing, he couldn't remember. More terrifying for him was that he didn't know who he was. Indeed, every twenty minutes or so, when he wasn't engaged in playing music or some such long-term activity, Mr. Wearing would suddenly come to life and feel his personal identity. He'd write in his journal or on some paper that he felt alive for the first time. Yet, after a few moments of consciousness, he'd forget once more who he was. Every time the musician "awoke" to his new identity, he'd read what he'd written the previous time and be unable to remember when he wrote it and how he felt when he wrote it. He even had no idea of who he was when he wrote it. So he'd be even more emphatic in writing that he was alive, to compensate in some way for the fact that he couldn't remember writing the previous statement or the emotion that attended it. Each time he "awoke," it felt new. So much for the self being present in feeling or thinking.

Even twenty years after the onset of the infection, Mr. Wearing is still unable to hold a unified consciousness over any length of time, although he now has some fragmentary grasp of what happened to him and what will occur to him when he lapses into "unconsciousness." He does, however, have a feeling about his life. It's a life without dreams or thoughts. For him, there is no difference between day or night, between the day before or the day to come. Neither sight nor sound means anything to him because there is nothing to compare them with or use them for. Twenty years later, he says, it still feels "just like death." One would be hard-pressed to come up with a more exquisite case of suffering than what Clive Wearing and those who love him have to put up with, over and over again.

Certainly, this musician's identity is tied up with some aspects of his memory. Ironically, when he's being the musician, and thus most fully recognizable as a functioning self and identifiable to those who knew him before his illness, he is only partly himself, even though he's performing and reading music and in every way seems to be in control of his surroundings. When, however, he is engaged directly—being stopped in the middle of conducting, or playing, or some such activity—he ceases to be recognizable as a functioning self and becomes unrecognizable. In other words, he is most himself when he is not; and most unlike himself when he is!

Yet, and this is the most outstanding and puzzling thing: somehow, behind his confusion, Mr. Wearing knows that he is *someone*, even when he doesn't not know who that someone is. He knows he loves his wife, who is still with him, even when he doesn't know the identity of this woman who calls herself his wife. Somehow, he understands that she is important to him. Naturally, it causes Mr. Wearing's wife great distress, because the musician greets her with great emotion each time he "awakes," as if after a long absence, even though she may have only gone out of the room for a few minutes. And, somehow, he knows that there is an "I" that "awakes" to life, one prior to the recovery of his memory—even though that "I" keeps on forgetting that it exists.

In short, Mr. Wearing is not, even to his wife, solely the sum of his broken, short-lived memories. While clearly this story shows that the memory has a powerful role in the creation of our identity, and the loss of it deeply affects our sense of who we are, this story and others like it that involve damage to parts of the brain only show how careful we should be in placing too much confidence in memory as the place where our identity exists. For, if Mr. Wearing's memory is so unreliable, then why does the "I" still persist in reminding itself of its existence? Perhaps, indeed, Mr. Wearing's twin selves—the long-term one and the short-term one—point to the conclusion that there is no single "I," but rather a collection of different identities that are present within our consciousness (or consciousnesses) at differing levels at different times throughout our lives.

In such a circumstance, therefore, we might ask: Who is the "I" that we awake to every morning? Where does *it* reside? Some have suggested that it is in our free will that our true identity resides. Yet, there are obvious problems here. None of us is completely free to do as we wish. In our daily life we're constantly confronted with limitations as to what we want to do, which is why we get angry when we cannot get what we want. Our boss may tell us to do something we don't want to do. Parents tell their children to study more but the children think they're being pushed too hard. In relationships also, the closer we are to someone, the more we want them to do what we want, and sometimes we get trapped because the other party doesn't cooperate. We certainly like to say we have free will, but experience tells us otherwise—that we're enmeshed in relationships with others and hidebound in our actions. Indeed, it would be impossible to imagine what it would be like to act entirely using our own free will; because everything we do is contingent on living in a society with others. It seems unlikely, then, that free will is where the self resides.

Perhaps it is with simple awareness that the self resides. I am aware of things around me, and aware of myself in that environment. Yet, this line of argument also falls down rapidly—especially when we remember the musician above and consider that, in a much less extreme situation, we aren't aware of who we are or where we are all the time. For instance, when we sleep our senses are quieted—we don't hear, see, smell, or sense anything. Likewise, people in a coma may not respond to anything. In sleep or in a coma, do we lose our self or our identity?

So the questions as to our identity remain, as they have been for centuries, open. Certainly, while these questions are intellectually intriguing, they're only of concern to Buddhism in as far as they can alleviate suffering. The suffering of the musician affected with short-term memory is acute, and it's hard for him not to feel enormous frustration at being unable to feel present through time. In a way that most of us can only begin to imagine he lives the condition of impermanence. His identity is only absolute to the extent that at certain moments throughout the day he feels fully aware of himself *for the first time*. But he knows that this condition is itself impermanent and this causes him great distress. Mr. Wearing gives us a glimpse into how frightening it is to discover that all those things we thought were permanent—including ourselves and our sense of our self—are, in fact, evanescent. We may feel as though we're disappearing, as though we're going insane. That's why it's so vital to recognize impermanence.

So how does Buddha talk about the self? Buddhism discusses this subject in terms of five aggregates, which every being possesses. These aggregates make up the physical body and the mental structure. The aggregates are our physical forms—eyes, ears, nose, tongue, body—our feelings, our perceptions, our volition or will power, and our consciousness. These aggregates constitute who we are.

Buddhism doesn't deny the existence of the empirical self. It agrees, for instance, with you when you feel that you are reading this book. Your body, feelings, perceptions, and volition *are* real. What Buddhism adds, however, is that the empirical self is *conditional*. In other words, it is like an onion. The onion is real, but if we peel the onion layer by layer we ultimately cannot find a core. However, although there is no core, we cannot deny the existence of the onion. Thus, the onion is conditional. And so are you. And so am I. What makes you and I present is the aggregation of numerous conditions. This is very important to understand. Non-Self, in Buddhism, doesn't necessarily mean no-self. The self, in Buddhism, is merely impermanent and interdependent. In the next chapter I discuss how such an understanding can help us guard against the effects of suffering.

10 ✻ Safeguarding the Heart

When we think of the suffering that affects so many people around the world in so many different ways, or that of Mr. Wearing and his wife, it's sometimes better for a moment to dwell in the moment and let that suffering sit with us. For all of the reality of interdependence, karma, and impermanence that I have discussed in the preceding pages, and for all of the space I have dedicated trying to point out how the self is impermanent and therefore it is wrong to cling too much to one's self-identity, it would be wrong if I didn't recognize how deep and entrenched suffering is in this world, and how tenacious is our need to cling to the self. Buddhism, as I have said, is founded on that recognition, and all Buddhists seek in their own ways to try to alleviate suffering, both for themselves and others. But, as it is necessary to remind ourselves over and over again, none of us should ever underestimate how hard that is to do.

It would be foolish to underestimate as well how hard it is for those who are suffering to see a way out. The memories of what happened to bring about that suffering—whether it is the loss of a loved one, physical hunger, a sense of hopelessness—may fade over the course of time; the images of the faces of the loved ones will be frozen in time, their complicated reality simplified by death, their faults forgotten and their lovable qualities enhanced. Distractions and new occurrences may also dilute the intensity of their absence, which may lead to guilt on behalf of the survivor or resentment on the part of the family if someone decides to move on with their life. The survivors and grieving family and friends may find other partners, friends, or move on; the children will grow, the buildings may be replaced or built over; people will forget what the memorials were for. But the suffering will still be there. It does not go away.

Therefore, for those who are suffering, Buddhism offers a simple counsel that acts as the first point of healing, a kind of triage for the individual. That counsel is to always safeguard the heart. We need to protect our heart from external or material damage and from the damage caused by anger, frustration, or fear. We need to protect it as if we were putting a sheet over it. If we do this, we are less likely to become lost in our suffering.

Anger is a particularly dangerous emotion for the heart.

It's a kind of double loss for the grieving or suffering person, because not only have we lost our loved one, but we now lose our heart. Anger merely allows the hurt feelings we have to become even more raw, hurting us more than it hurts the one who caused us pain. Once more, this is very hard. Anger is a natural reaction. For Buddhists, however, the task throughout our lives is to become aware of emotions such as anger and watch our mind as the emotions well up. Our challenge is to protect our hearts from the damage these emotions can inflict. Anger leads to blind acts of hate. Anger makes people sacrifice their own lives to kill other people, simply because they might belong to the same group as the one they perceive hurt them. As we've seen over the last few years, this cycle of violence only continues and exacerbates the suffering, as retribution and revenge are enacted in ever more gruesome ways, and more and more people are subjected to the pain and in turn experience anger and hatred that causes them to seek revenge. As Mahatma Gandhi once said, "An eye for an eye leaves the whole world blind." Looking at a terrible event from a wider perspective enables us not to excuse what happened but to place what happened within a broad context where all of us act, both for good and for bad, in an infinitely complex, interlocking system of cause and effect. In sum, while we may witness the suffering, we must make sure that before we do anything we do not become its victims, by safeguarding the heart.

Religious institutions can offer comfort to the brokenhearted, but I always say that it is not so much the temple or church where enlightenment or comfort takes place, it is the mind. This is not to downgrade the importance of such institutions or the charity they can afford. After all, there need to be the material conditions for reflection to take place: the victim who suffers needs to have physical and material help, and we should rejoice at the generosity that many people show in the wake of general tragedy, or any of the countless individual tragedies that occur each day. Moreover, safeguarding the heart is not something we need to be a Buddhist to undertake. Buddhism is not a secret truth. The Truth has always been there; it is simply that the Buddha pointed it out. But without the right mental preparation to provide counsel and comfort, then true healing will not take place, no matter under which religious doctrine or in what location that counsel or comfort is offered.

In order to guard our heart we need to practice awareness. By watching our thoughts and emotions, we can guard against, literally, losing our mind. Practicing awareness is like an ox herder watching his oxen. He needs to keep an eye on his oxen or they will wander off beyond his fields. We need to control our mind so it doesn't become wild. Indeed, the very act of watching the mind can bring it back into balance. Balance is very important here. If there is too much sorrow in our mind, we need to bring some kind of joy into it to balance it. When there is too much levity, we need to make it more serene and calm. When we're very angry, we need to cool the mind down. When the mind is indifferent, we need to inject it with passion.

In order for us to balance the mind it is important to know what our mental state is. Many of us who let the mind go wild don't know we're unhappy or angry or depressed. We haven't taken time to monitor our mental state. So the first thing we need to do is to know our state of mind. This is why I say it is necessary to guard our heart from anger. Until we know what we're feeling, how can we protect ourselves from the consequences of that feeling? The point of knowing what we're feeling is not to deny those feelings. Anger is a genuine emotion; stifling it will not give us any relief. It will merely emerge in some other direction. Yet, simply observing the anger in and of itself will provide some sense of how we deal with the emotion. And one of the great lessons of Buddhism is the use of meditation to do just that.

Meditation offers an opportunity to still mental anguish through the safeguarding of our heart from negative emotions. Meditation is like a security guard monitoring who is coming in and going out of a building. Meditation observes the thoughts—whether they're good, bad, or neutral. Buddhism has two kinds of meditation, which are really part of the same thing. One is called *samatha* (Sanskrit, *samadhi*) and the other is *vipassana* (in Sanskrit, *vipasyana*). In Chinese, we call the first the meditation on calmness and stillness; the second we call the meditation on insight and contemplation.

To use an analogy I employed earlier on in this book,

samatha meditation practice involves allowing the glass of murky water to be stilled and the water to settle. In other words, disturbed feelings that cloud our reason and confuse our sense of what we need to do should be allowed to calm down so that our reason becomes clearer and the way forward more transparent. By watching our anger, for instance, we can control it by at least being able to acknowledge that we *want* to watch our anger. Meditation allows us not to be overwhelmed by the emotion and instead to ask ourselves what we're angered by, whom we're angry with, and why. *Vipassana* meditation then follows up these questions by asking how the anger comes about and why it is affecting us. We're then able to ask how the anger is helping or disabling us and how we can let it go away.

Both forms of meditation need to work together. If we're so overwhelmed and overtaken by anger, we won't be able to ask the questions of how the anger happens and why it's affecting us. We'll be so wrapped up in the emotion—in wanting to hurt someone or hurt ourselves—that we won't care why we're feeling what we're feeling. We won't want to hear any other options, even the ones that are speaking to us from our gut. So, the calmness and stillness brought about by the first form of meditation is essential for the emotions to be brought back from being too overwhelming. Once the mind is stilled, it's possible to answer the questions of the second stage. Only when we've calmed ourselves can we ask the questions: Why do good people die young? Why did this happen? What will happen to me in the future? How are we going to deal with our anger? Will anger help us?

You'll remember that earlier on I compared reality to looking in a mirror; these two meditations function in the same way. In *samatha* meditation, we polish the mirror so that we can see things clearly, which is a function of *vipassana* meditation. The mirror that we polish not only reflects back to us things we didn't see clearly because we hadn't disciplined the mind, but it opens up the areas behind us so we can see more clearly the causes and effects of our feelings. Moreover, with a polished mirror we now don't see things narrowly, but we can see things more widely. We can look at the mirror from any angle, opening up to our view more visions previously hidden from us.

When we've gone through the process of stilling and then examining the mind, what occurs is not indifference but compassion. This is activated by our sense of karma, of how we're all linked together. Once we realize our interconnectedness, that all things have an effect, both long- and short-term—and that the things we do, individually and collectively, have an effect perhaps in ways we couldn't have imagined because we remained blinkered by our own cultural, religious, or other conditioning—then we can all contribute our part. As I pointed out earlier, the wound that another individual experiences becomes our wound; their suffering our suffering.

Likewise, our healing becomes their healing, the alleviation of our suffering the alleviation of theirs.

In such circumstances, therefore, not only does the suffering person need healing, but we *all* need healing—and it is everyone's responsibility to undertake that healing. However, if we focus solely on individual cases and ignore the larger connection, and consequently consider only revenge as the option for action, then we'll cause more hatred and hurt—to ourselves and others. To return to the medical analogy used earlier, if we merely try and excise the wound without realizing how it came about, then we'll simply spread the infection to other parts so that the wound becomes worse.

That said, we should be aware of the pressure on us, and the pressure we place on others, to alleviate suffering. Sometimes, we burden ourselves too greatly, and that only leads us to become weighed down and thus, paradoxically, less able to help reduce the suffering. I think about a green apple on the tree. The apple possesses the final shape it is going to be, it is even the same size; but it is not ripe. Sometimes, we need to sit and let time work its course for something to come to fruition. We're often too impatient to have things done, and have things brought to their completion—even when we're acting against the natural, physical laws of the universe.

There is a story about a Buddhist sage that I touched upon earlier that exemplifies our carrying around of burdens. One day, the sage and a disciple came to a riverbank where there was a young woman trying to cross the river. She was, however, unable to walk through the swollen tide and asked the sage to help. In spite of vows that commanded him not to touch women, the sage picked up the woman and carried her across the river on his back. Once they'd reached the other side of the river, the sage lowered the woman to the ground. She thanked him profusely and bade him farewell. The disciple was shocked by the sage's breaking of his vow, but said nothing. After three months, the disciple could stand it no more. He went to the sage and reproached him for breaking his vow by touching a woman. The sage laughed: "I merely carried the burden of this woman for the length of time it took to cross a river; yet you have been burdened by it for more than three months. Who has been more errant from his vows?"

What this story tells us is that we cannot freight our deeds with meaning when the meaning itself will weigh us down. If we do good, we need to act without expectations of reward or revenge or recognition. If we do so, the karma of our thoughts will not go against the karma of our deeds.

11 ❈ The Four Diligences

Before detailing the power of meditation as a practical method to help relieve suffering, I need to point out the Four Diligences, which are key components of meditation. Of the Four Diligences, two deal with good thoughts, and two with bad. Both of them are balanced contrasts, although in practice they're deeply interwoven.

The first diligence is to prevent bad thoughts arising in the first place. The second diligence is to deal with the bad thoughts once they've arisen by eliminating them. The third diligence is to generate good thoughts if they've not arisen, while the fourth diligence is to nourish those good thoughts if they've arisen and make them stronger and more substantial. The Four Diligences are directly applicable to the ego and desire. Our relationships are often begun out of desire, where we know a relationship won't work but want to try it for a short time to see what it will be like. Many times we pay for our indulgence. We need to have the strength and self-knowledge to examine our thoughts as they arise to see what desires, cravings, attachments, or impulses lie behind them and whether they're good or bad thoughts.

These diligences apply not only to human relationships but our relationships with all things. For instance, some people tell me I am a high-tech nun because I use computers. I like using faxes, digital cameras, camcorders, cellular phones, and other mechanical objects because they're efficient and make our life easier. But I don't want machines to rule our lives or make life more complicated by having to rely on them. We have to remember that we invented the machines and not they us!

One of the central problems I believe confronting contemporary society is that we don't practice the Four Diligences enough. We rush headlong into acquiring things, relationships, and technology without wondering whether we really need them or want them for our own selfish purposes rather than generating good. I understand that talk about the dissolute life tends to be filled with clichés—drugs, women, marital problems, the high life. Unfortunately, however, there is some truth in clichés. Rarely do we want to count the true costs of our attachments and desires, but count them we have to eventually, if not in this lifetime then in the lifetimes to come.

How do we apply the Four Diligences to something

such as anger? When we encounter something that upsets us, we need to tell ourselves not to let the anger hurt us first. You may have received a letter in which somebody slanders or rejects you. Or your lover may have written you a letter where he or she is telling you they're breaking up with you. Therefore, you get angry. The first thing we need to do is to keep ourselves calm and give ourselves constructive thoughts. We keep ourselves calm by not allowing the disturbing thoughts to arise or, should we begin to feel ourselves getting angry, by diverting those angry thoughts and, as it were, detaching ourselves from them. We should tell ourselves we're not going to let the anger hurt us.

The second step is to tell ourselves that we're going to deal with this matter calmly and wisely. In order to do this, we need to have positive and wholesome thoughts inside us before dealing with the outside matter. Sometimes, it may not be enough to tell ourselves to stop being angry and the anger disappears. It may not be that easy. If we need to go shopping or listen to music, then that is fine. But the *thought* behind the action is very important. Don't let the anger hurt you. You must think calmly and wisely.

Buddhist understanding of who we are and what our relationship is to the outside world is particularly useful in helping us deal with anger. Frustration occurs because we're not aware of, and are not prepared for, change. When we get frustrated with our relationships, our family, school, society, our financial status, and career, it is because, as I have said, everything is changing. Therefore, Buddhism teaches the concept of dependent origination—of everything involved with everything else. I couldn't have done what I did without others. Nor could you. If we only saw life in this way, we'd be able to appreciate how much we have.

Dealing with our thoughts requires awareness, before any action can take place. I always say that the mind is our fate. Some people when they encounter frustration are able to reconstruct their thoughts as to how they became frustrated in the first place. But many of us allow the mind and our thoughts to overwhelm us and let the thoughts lead us wherever they like. We need to be aware of our thoughts, so that when they're good we can let them flourish and when they're bad we can remove them. It is like a seed, planted in the ground. If it is left alone, the seed will tend to flourish and grow. If the seed is good, then it should be nurtured. But if the seed is bad then we need to uproot it. However, the best method is to be aware that the thought is bad at the beginning, before it's planted. Otherwise, if we're not aware and let the thought grow like a big tree and try to get rid of it, then the task is much harder. Not only do we have to chop off the branches and cut through the trunk, but we still have to deal with the roots that need to be dug out. And this is how habits and addictions are formed. We may get rid of the visible manifestation of our bad thoughts, but we've not addressed the root causes of those thoughts. Consequently, soon enough, the bad thoughts begin to sprout again.

Meditation is the discipline and training whereby we prepare the ground for the good thoughts and develop the tools to resist the bad. Because we live in a world where we're so easily distracted, where our mind is always wandering around outside our heads, as it were, it may take some time and effort to learn to control the oxen! We're bombarded by images that stimulate our minds into frenzied activities. The first act of meditation should be to remove ourselves from external stimulation and draw the mind inward. This step is then followed by the meditator asking him- or herself a fundamental question: "What are you thinking?" Observe yourself and your thoughts. Examine what thoughts you're thinking, what is in your mind at that moment. The idea at this point is not to change those thoughts necessarily, but merely to examine what they are. This is called cultivating awareness, and it is the essential mechanism of meditation.

(One further statement that needs to be made before I discuss the processes of meditation is that meditation doesn't mean sitting down in a temple or a church. It can be done anywhere, even when we're walking along. At every moment during the day, we can ask ourselves what we're thinking. Nevertheless, given that most people when they think about meditation think it is about sitting still, I will concentrate on sitting meditation. As a basic technique, sitting meditation is, indeed, extremely effective.)

There are three elements to meditation. The first element is body posture. We need to sit erect but relaxed. We might cross our legs fully in the lotus position, or if we're not supple enough for this position yet we may sit in the half-lotus position. I recommend the latter for those who are older or for people in physical discomfort. It's important that you feel comfortable and relaxed.

When you're in this position, you should do an inventory of your body from the top of your head to the bottom of your toes and check each part of the body to make sure every muscle is relaxed. First, you should relax the top of the head and then the forehead. If you're frowning, release the frown. If your cheeks are tense, then smile a little. Place your tongue against the roof of the mouth behind the teeth. Open or close your eyes as you wish, as long as closing your eyes won't make you drowsy. The important thing is to become aware and not fall asleep! Then you should concentrate on following all of the muscles down the body, placing your mind in that area of the body and checking to see whether the muscles are relaxed or tense. Join your palms together, with the tips of your thumbs connecting and the fingers interlaced. Sit upright, not in a fixed, rigid position but comfortably. Your spine should be straight and not hunched over.

The second element in meditation is breathing. A standard technique for breathing is counting each breath as it goes in and each breath as it goes out. On the first in- and out-breath you should count to one. On the second in- and out-breath you should count to two. On the third, count to three, and so on up to ten. Then you should return to one, and then two, etc. The slower you can do this, the better, although you shouldn't try and force yourself beyond your natural breathing patterns. Once again, the point is to become conscious of your breathing rather than simply holding your breath. It is preferable to allow the fresh air that is breathed in down through the lungs to go right into the abdomen and then to bring the stale breath from inside the body out through the nose.

The next element of the breathing technique is to focus on the breathing itself. You should be aware of the air as it enters your nostrils and goes down into the body and then as it comes back out of the body. Don't try and breathe in too much air or make too much of an effort. Simply breathing rhythmically and consciously is already awareness in action and will aid you in your concentration. You can use this technique to quell your anger or to safeguard your heart or even when you are nervous because you are meeting someone important or are about to do something dangerous. By not letting our mind get distracted and focusing on the breathing, you can lower your heart rate, oxygenate the blood, and let your mind rest for a while.

By observing your breathing you're automatically controlling your thought patterns. This is the third element of meditation. Controlling thought patterns is all about avoiding distractions and learning to concentrate. To do this, you need to be aware of breathing and focus on certain bodily sensations.

The effect can be extraordinary. When I became a nun,
nearly three decades ago, I had an ulcer that I had had for
several years from before I entered the monastery. An en-
doscopy revealed that I had two small holes in the lining of
my stomach. One night, the pain was excruciating and I sat
up and began to meditate. After adjusting my posture and beginning to breathe consciously I began to focus on the two
holes. I brought all my energy to bear on them. I tried to
pinpoint the pain, moving my mind around the area where
it hurt. The strange thing was that the more I examined the
area the more I realized that the pain was moving. I couldn't
locate the exact source. In addition, I was trying to work out
what I felt exactly—what the nature of the pain was. We
often say that we feel pain, but we often cannot describe what
the pain really is. I wanted to find out the essence of the pain.
So, as I sat and tried not only to locate the pain but to determine its nature, I discovered that the pain had vanished. What
I realized was that the pain was conditioned, and that once I
brought my focus to the pain, the pain revealed itself to be
nothing in and of itself and disappeared. I had peeled away
each layer of pain until there was nothing at the core. After
that meditation, I cured the ulcer, and I've not taken medicine for many, many years.

Now, while this discovery was extraordinary for me, it
was not miraculous. In fact, it was profoundly rational. My
thought was: I have two holes in the wall of my stomach; I
need to mend them. I used my thoughts and their energies

as a kind of healing medication to repair the holes. In Chinese acupuncture, practitioners talk of the "acupuncture of the will." What they mean is that, while the doctors may use physical needles to stimulate the energy that might heal the wound, the other needle that has to be employed for healing to take place is the will.

Meditation has the power to activate the will and focus it very effectively. I'm not advocating its suitability for all ailments, especially very serious diseases or illnesses, but the focused mind is a powerful tool. Meditation will not stop suffering—as we have seen, nothing can. However, meditation can provide us with a way to lessen the by-products of suffering, such as anger, frustration, or fear. In such a way, meditation enables us to look more clearly upon the causes of suffering and spend our lives dedicated to lessening it—for ourselves and for all sentient beings.

Conclusion

Tragedies happen every day. Buddhism doesn't offer easy solutions or emotional palliatives. Instead, it realistically responds to suffering—both in our own lives and in the lives of others—and demands that we do something about it. It does so in compassion and with the recognition that we're far from perfect; it does so acknowledging that we'll never be perfect while we think we *can* be perfect. Buddhism can be harsh; but then so can pain, and so can responsibility. We cannot merely hope for suffering to end or wait around for others to end it for us. If we do, we'll be hoping in vain and waiting for an eternity. Buddhism provides a way of engaging that promises liberation for all of us because our destinies are bound up with all the other beings who share this planet—whether they be our families, those who seek to destroy our way of life, those who rescue us from the flames, and those countless others whose names and lives we will never know.

As I hope this book has shown, life is very fragile and precious, and our time on Earth demands not resignation or forgetfulness but mindfulness and engagement. It teaches us that there is beauty even in the midst of horror, but only if we work for the good of all rather than the particular interests of the few. It asks us to commit to what seems impossible—a life dedicated to the helping of others who don't belong to our family but to the family of Man, and then beyond that to the families of all beings who live and die and live again on this small blue orb in the three layers of the thousand worlds.

Suffering cannot be eliminated at one time or by all sentient beings. It will occur over a long period of time and very suddenly. Buddhism sees this reality. As I was once told by my dear friend Dr. William Ury, who helped create the Global Negotiation Project at Harvard University, we cannot expect to resolve or eliminate all conflicts. However, he continued, the most important thing is to become aware of our attitude toward those conflicts. As we have seen—in events as cataclysmic as a tidal wave, as shocking as September 11, and as random as the shootings at Virginia Tech—we need to be mindful of cause and effect, reach out and offer our help and condolences, and safeguard the heart.

Appendix ❋ Humanistic Buddhism

In 1979, a friend took me to a Buddhist monastery in my native Taiwan for a retreat. I saw it more as an opportunity to have a vacation, with free board and lodging, and thought no more of it. However, the monastery—the Fo Guang Shan temple—taught me meditation and chanting, and helped me realize that Buddhism was not superstition or only for old people, as I had previously thought, but was practical and contemporary. I joined as soon as I could, and through the institution undertook further studies in law and Buddhist philosophy, and I have been with the temple, both in the United States and Taiwan, ever since.

Fo Guang Shan's founder was Venerable Master Hsing Yun, who became a Buddhist monk at age twelve. He fled to Taiwan from mainland China in 1949, and founded the Fo

Guang Shan International Buddhist Order soon afterwards.
There are now hundreds of temples all over the world, in-
cluding in Asia, the United States, Europe, Central and South
America, Africa, and Australia. Although we practice Chan
Buddhism (the Chinese form of Zen Buddhism), Master
Hsing Yun has named his particular school Humanistic Bud-
dhism.

Humanistic Buddhism has six main characteristics. The
first is its emphasis on the human nature of the Buddha.
Sakyamuni Buddha, the founder of Buddhism, was a living
human being, born in this world, with a family, and a real life.
He attained his enlightenment in this world. He was not a divine being or the Creator. He proclaimed that he was a dis-
coverer who found the path that he shared with the ancient
sages. Humanistic Buddhism emphasizes the Buddha's hu-
manity because it shows that we can all be compassionate,
ethical, and use intuitive wisdom as he did.

The second characteristic is Humanistic Buddhism's
emphasis on daily life. The Buddha gave very specific instructions on how we should live our daily life, and Humanistic
Buddhism advocates following those instructions. We experience the suffering in our daily life, and we need to eliminate
it in our everyday life. The wisdom is to apply the Buddhist
values and ethic in our daily life.

The third characteristic is altruism—that we always
keep in mind how we can help and best serve others. We cannot live isolatedly when the Buddha taught us the interde-

pendence of all beings. A Buddha, the Enlightened One, cannot reach his goal by separating himself from all the sentient beings. We cannot reach our happiness while the rest of the world is suffering.

The fourth characteristic is joyfulness. Our aim is to provide joy through the relief of suffering for all sentient beings. The goal for Buddhists is the cessation of the suffering. It is very important to bring joy not only to one's own self but also to others. Meditation and contemplation are used to eliminate the negative thoughts with which we harm ourselves.

The fifth characteristic is timeliness. Humanistic Buddhism seeks to make Buddhism meaningful and relevant for today's spiritual seekers. We adopt the values and principles of Buddhism to examine the current social issues and advocate peaceful, nonviolent solutions. Humanistic Buddhism works to build a heaven–like pure land on this earth. When we take good care in this life, this moment, we're not worried about the life after death.

The sixth characteristic is universality. The wisdom of the Buddha is not under the exclusive control of a group of people, nor does his wisdom only apply to a few. It applies to all beings, because he wished to save all beings. Humanistic Buddhism believes that all the sentient beings embrace the potential for enlightenment, regardless of social status, race, gender, or even species.

Humanistic Buddhism provides a dynamic form of

contemporary Buddhism that promotes compassion and wisdom, is practical in orientation and is open to everyone, no
matter their background or religious affiliation.

About the Venerable Yifa

Venerable Yifa has been a nun at Fo Guang Shan Monastery in Taiwan since 1979. She received a law degree from the National Taiwan University, an M.A. in comparative philosophy from the University of Hawaii, and her Ph.D. in religious studies from Yale University in 1996. She was named one of the "Ten Outstanding Young Persons" in Taiwan in 1997. She has been a visiting scholar at the University of California at Berkeley and Harvard University, a lecturer at Boston University, and a faculty member at the National Sun Yat-Sen University in Taiwan. She has also been Dean at Fo Guang Shan Buddhist College and Provost at Hsi Lai University, Rosemead, California. In 2005, she taught at McGill University as the Numata visiting professor, and was until recently Chair of the Department of Religious Studies at the University of the West in Los Angeles. In Bangkok in 2003, she was awarded the United Nations "Outstanding Women in Buddhism Award." Since 2002, Venerable Yifa has conducted the Humanistic Buddhist Monastic Life Program (also called the "Woodenfish Program") for teens and college students, sponsored by Buddha's Light International Society, and more recently has been the director of the Buddha's Light Sutra Translation Center, set up to research and translate Buddhist scriptures. For many years Venerable Yifa has been engaged in interfaith dialogues such as the "Gethsemane Encounter," "International Buddhist–Christian Theology," and "Religious Ethics," supported by UNESCO. She co-chaired "Nuns in the West," an interfaith monastic dialogue, and was a contributor to the "Safe Motherhood Project" by UNICEF's South Asia office. She is the author of *The Origin of Buddhist Monastic Codes in China* (Hawaii University Press, 2002), *Safeguarding the Heart: A Buddhist Response to Suffering and September 11* (Lantern Books, 2002), *Authenticity* (Lantern Books, 2007), *The Tender Heart* (Lantern Books, 2007), *Discernment* (Lantern Books, 2008), and *Sisters of the Buddha* (Lantern Books, 2008).

Also by Yifa:

Authenticity
978-1-59056-109-6
Venerable Yifa explores junk in all its ramifications: junk food, junk stuff, junk relationships, junk communication, and junk thoughts and feelings. She shows how our obsession with materialism, convenience, and the fast-paced nature of our society is diminishing our ability to connect wholeheartedly with others and making it harder for us to lead authentic lives.

Discernment
978-1-59056-121-8
In *Discernment*, the Venerable Yifa explores some of the central concerns of Buddhism—the nature of suffering, impermanence, the laws of cause and effect, and the nature of the individual—unpacking some of the subtler dimensions of these popular Buddhist stories. In so doing, she shows how Buddhism relates to contemporary life.

Sisters of the Buddha
978-1-59056-059-4
Like all other world religions, Buddhism has had its share of controversies regarding women's roles. Yifa, looks at the role of women in early Buddhism, appraises the controversial "eight rules" that women have to obey in order to become Buddhist nuns and examines the social conditions of women throughout the Buddhist world. Yifa concentrates on the still largely unknown Chinese tradition, bringing to light new insights into this important strand of Buddhist culture and the women who were embedded in it. Using her twenty-year experience as a Buddhist nun, Yifa reveals the opportunities and challenges that await any woman who seeks to become a Buddhist, and in so doing uncovers the heart of the spiritual calling.

To order visit www.lanternbooks.com.